A Camper's Guide to
Ontario's Best Parks

A Camper's Guide to
Ontario's Best Parks

Donna Carpenter

The BOSTON
MILLS PRESS

CANADIAN CATALOGUING IN
PUBLICATION DATA

Carpenter, Donna May Gibbs, 1954–
A camper's guide to Ontario's best parks

ISBN 1-55046-315-2

1. Camping — Ontario — Guidebooks.
2. National parks and reserves — Ontario —
Guidebooks. 3. Provincial parks and reserves —
Ontario — Guidebooks. 4. Natural resources
conservation areas — Ontario — Guidebooks.
5. Ontario. Guidebooks. I. Title

FC3063.C37 2000   796.5409713
C00-930448-7
F1011.C37 2000

Published in 2000 by
BOSTON MILLS PRESS
132 Main Street
Erin, Ontario N0B 1T0
Tel 519-833-2407
Fax 519-833-2195
e-mail books@bostonmillspress.com
www.bostonmillspress.com

An affiliate of
STODDART PUBLISHING CO. LIMITED
34 Lesmill Road
Toronto, Ontario, Canada
M3B 2T6
Tel 416-445-3333
Fax 416-445-5967
e-mail gdsinc@genpub.com

Distributed in Canada by
GENERAL DISTRIBUTION SERVICES
LIMITED
325 Humber College Boulevard
Toronto, Canada M9W 7C3
Orders 1-800-387-0141 Ontario & Quebec
Orders 1-800-387-0172 NW Ontario
& other provinces
e-mail cservice@genpub.com

Distributed in the United States by
GENERAL DISTRIBUTION SERVICES
INC.
PMB 128, 4500 Witmer Industrial Estates
Niagara Falls, New York 14305-1386
Toll-free 1-800-805-1083
Toll-free fax 1-800-481-6207
e-mail gdsinc@genpub.com
www.genpub.com

Design by Mary Firth
Cover design by Gillian Stead and Mary Firth
Printed in Canada

THE CANADA COUNCIL | LE CONSEIL DES ARTS
FOR THE ARTS | DU CANADA
SINCE 1957 | DEPUIS 1957

We acknowledge for their financial support of our
publishing program the Canada Council, the
Ontario Arts Council, and the Government of
Canada through the Book Publishing Industry
Development Program (BPIDP).

Contents

Central Ontario

Southwestern Ontario

Introduction

Ontario enjoys a remarkable natural heritage. In our public parks you can partake of such diverse delights as Algonquin's wolf-howl excursions, a top-of-the-world view from the Sleeping Giant, Arrowhead's exhilarating toboggan run, and the northern lights over Nagagamisis. Our equally fascinating cultural heritage, from Agawa's red pictographs to voyageur canoes travelling the Mattawa River, comes to life in the creative programs offered in many parks.

Ontario has hundreds of parks to choose from. Most come under one of three different administrations: the national parks, provincial parks or conservation areas. Consider the number of different park types and then factor in the variety of Ontario's physical landscape and you are left with a mind-boggling array of park experiences to choose from. Selecting a park for quality campsites, facilities, scenery and location is not an easy task. This book can help you identify which of these parks is just right for your needs. One of these could become your next home away from home.

How to Use This Book

A Camper's Guide to Ontario's Best Parks can help you choose a park for your next camping trip. Forty-five of Ontario's best parks are described under the headings of natural environment and history, special activities, campgrounds and local attractions.

If you have a preference for a particular kind of scenery—beaches or mountains, for instance—then read the *natural environment and history* section of a park description. It is a good guide to the size of the park and its general landscape. The *special activities* descriptions highlight the best ways to enjoy each park. Information on hiking and ski trails, boating, fishing and interpretive programs is found in this section.

The *campgrounds* section gives the number of campsites, the number of sites with hydro hookups, and recommends the "best" sites in each campground. The sites recommended here are usually the most private and quiet, with a good vegetation buffer surrounding the site. The *local attractions* section of the park description identifies local villages, museums, events and activities that are worth including in your travel plans. Park staff are usually good sources of ideas on the best tourist resources in their region.

Parks Listed in This Book

A Camper's Guide to Ontario's Best Parks describes only those parks that offer camping; thus, day-use parks are not discussed. Although canoe tripping and long-distance hiking are popular activities, bookstores already provide guidebooks that address the needs of wilderness adventurers. Thus, while opportunities for hike-in or paddle-in camping are mentioned, this book is best for campers who are looking for a good campground accessible by car.

This book identifies parks within each geographic region of the province and within each of our different natural landscapes. In addition, there are listings for excellent parks close to every major community in the province.

Ontario has about 10 or 12 parks that have celebrity status; these are very heavily used from spring to fall. Off-season, the most popular parks can offer superior camping experiences. However, during the prime season, from mid-July to mid-August, you could have a better park visit if you opt to camp in one of our lesser-known parks. Your decision will be rewarded with a better campsite, more privacy and quiet, and an equally beautiful park.

Each of the 45 parks described in this book is rated according to natural environment, activities and campground. The rating system is 1, 2, 3, with 1 the lowest rating and 3 the highest rating. The natural environment rating refers to the scenic beauty of a park. The activities rating describes three features: interpretive programming, diversity of opportunities for outdoor pursuits, and the number of top-notch local attractions. The campground rating refers to the privacy and size of campsites.

Campsite Reservations

All good camping trips require advance planning. And in the face of the increasing popularity of Ontario's parks, campsite reservations are a good means of ensuring the success of your expedition. Reservations are especially advisable at all of Ontario's most popular parks.

The type of park you are visiting determines how you may reserve a campsite. In the case of national parks and conservation areas, sites may be reserved by a telephone call to the park office. Phone numbers are provided with each park description.

The Province of Ontario has an excellent telephone reservation system that serves most provincial parks listed in this book. The central reservation number is 888-668-7275. This central reservation system operates 24 hours a day. You may reserve a specific site in many parks up to 11 months in advance. When you call the provincial park reservation system, it is useful to be prepared with the following information:

Credit card number and expiry date
Dates of arrival/departure
Park of interest
Campsite of interest (or at least a description of site requirements, such as whether you require a hydro hookup, want to be in a radio-free zone, need to be close to a comfort station, and so on)

Camping equipment (in other words, are you tenting, towing a trailer or driving a motorhome?)
Home address and telephone number

Some parks, mainly more remote or lesser-used parks, are not part of this central reservation service. Sites at these parks are given out on a first-come, first-served basis. Many of the parks that accept reservations also hold a small number of sites for allocation on a first-come, first-served basis.

Roofed Accommodation and Other Rentals

In response to consumer interest in "soft adventure," the Ontario government has created a variety of roofed accommodations in many provincial parks. These accommodations rent at very reasonable rates, and are especially ideal when cool spring or fall weather can make tent camping unappealing.

One of the most common alternatives is the "yurt." Yurts are canvas structures on a wood platform, furnished with a fully equipped kitchen, beds for up to six people, and other necessities. Yurts occupy regular campsites and include a gas barbecue.

Some provincial parks rent cabins on a per-night or weekly basis. Some of these cabins are former cottages, staff houses or remote forest-ranger cabins. Larger groups may rent bunkhouses or lodges that are available in a few provincial parks.

Each park description in this book notes what type of roofed accommodation, if any, is available. Reservations for roofed accommodation are handled through the central reservation system.

Ontario's provincial parks are going out of their way to make camping as convenient as possible. Most parks rent canoes and some parks also rent boats, paddleboats, kayaks, bicycles and cross-country skis. A small number of parks rent tents and other necessities, and store trailers and boats off-season. Each park description notes the type of outdoor or sports equipment rented at each park. For information on camping equipment rentals, please contact the park you are interested in visiting.

Camping in Ontario's wonderful parks is a great way to enjoy a holiday, travel across the province and soak up some backcountry solitude. Be sure to put a park on your next travel itinerary.

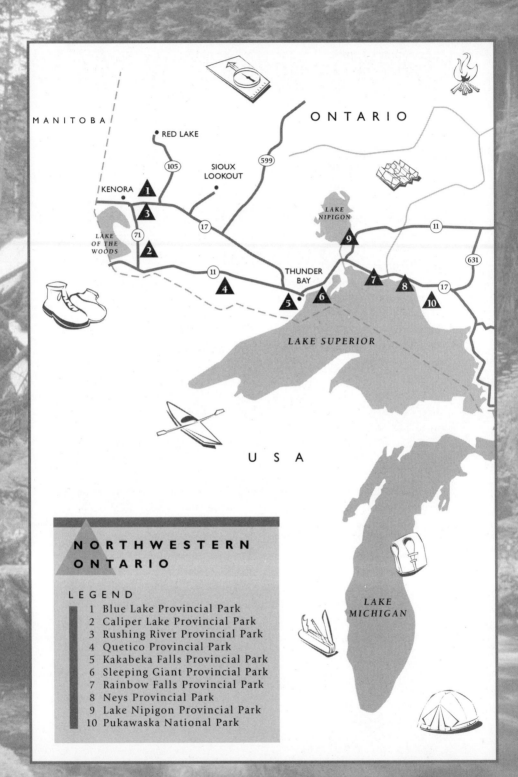

MANITOBA

ONTARIO

RED LAKE

105

SIOUX
LOOKOUT

599

KENORA

1

3

LAKE
NIPIGON

11

71

LAKE
OF THE
WOODS

17

9

631

2

11

THUNDER
BAY

7

4

17

5

6

8

10

LAKE SUPERIOR

USA

LAKE
MICHIGAN

NORTHWESTERN ONTARIO

LEGEND
1 Blue Lake Provincial Park
2 Caliper Lake Provincial Park
3 Rushing River Provincial Park
4 Quetico Provincial Park
5 Kakabeka Falls Provincial Park
6 Sleeping Giant Provincial Park
7 Rainbow Falls Provincial Park
8 Neys Provincial Park
9 Lake Nipigon Provincial Park
10 Pukawaska National Park

Northwestern Ontario

Blue Lake Provincial Park

Location: 11 km off Highway 17, 48 km northwest of Dryden.
Natural Environment: 2 **Activities:** 2 **Campground:** 1

If you were to ask park enthusiasts in Northwestern Ontario what was their favourite destination for family enjoyment, Blue Lake would top the list. Blue Lake Provincial Park encompasses two lakes, Blue and Langton, and the height of land between them. The object of everyone's affection is Blue Lake, loved for its remarkable colour, clarity and striking beauty. Combine the lake's natural attraction with a broad beach, an interpretive program geared to visitors of all ages, and several pretty but non-strenuous hiking trails, and you have the making of a great family getaway.

Natural Environment and History

Blue Lake, a remnant of glacial Lake Agassiz, is not only spectacularly blue, but its water is so clear that you can easily see to a depth of 6 m. Another characteristic equally uncommon for a northern lake is the amount of fine sand distributed along the shoreline.

The lake is set within typical northern boreal forest of black spruce, red and jack pine with areas of aspen and white birch. The wildlife inhabiting Blue Lake's forests is also typical of Northern Ontario, but includes animals not seen by many Ontarians: spruce grouse, boreal chorus frog, fox and hare, for example. Wildflowers abound here; especially interesting are carnivorous pitcher plants and lady's-slipper orchid. Wild blueberries are a popular reason for midsummer family outings.

Special Activities

Blue Lake has a large, loyal following of families, many of whom have spent their summer holidays here annually for decades. The main attraction is the beautiful beach of water-rippled sand that extends far along the shore and into the lake. It's perfect for wading youngsters. The water's clarity means that this is one of the few parks in Northwestern Ontario where snorkelling and scuba diving are worthwhile pursuits.

There are other ways to enjoy the water at Blue Lake. Boaters appreciate the boat launch located near the beach. Canoeing is especially rewarding, since Blue Lake has many connecting waterways that lead to small lakes with calm waters and few visitors. The privately run store just outside the park boundary rents canoes, boats and paddleboats. There's fishing for pickerel, pike, muskie and lake trout on Blue Lake.

Next to watersports, hiking is the most common pastime at Blue Lake. Each of the four short trails has its own interpretive brochure. On the Spruce Fen Trail you walk to a fen, a wetland where plants form a living, floating mat over acidic waters. This barrier-free 2-km boardwalk crosses a beaver pond and is the easiest way to study intriguing northern wetlands. The brochure for the one-kilometre-long Boulder Ridge Trail describes glacial ridges and rivers seen en route as well as the ecology of fire-maintained jack pine forests. The most popular trail is the 4-km Rock Point Trail, which leads through cedar forest and jack pine highlands to Langton Lake. Eight-kilometre-long Blue Lake to Goblin Lake Trail follows the shoreline of Blue Lake to a tiny, quiet interior lake.

Blue Lake park staff have a reputation for friendly service. Their interpretive program includes presentations in the amphitheatre about local plants and animals. The program also features guided hikes, slide shows and movies, spirit hikes (where staff members in costume take on the roles of figures from park history), canoe hikes, blueberry-picking walks and archaeological digs. Events are usually scheduled for each mid-morning, mid-afternoon and evening, and activities are family oriented. The park nature centre has displays on park ecology and a children's nature library; staff in the centre are available to answer questions and to help plan backcountry outings.

During the winter, Blue Lake Provincial Park is a preferred destination for snowmobilers and cross-country skiers. The park rents a 16-person, fully equipped and heated cabin to groups wanting to stay overnight in the park during the off-season.

Campground

Blue Lake has 196 campsites, 42 with electrical connections. Many sites are designed as pull-throughs for trailers. There is very little to choose between the sites at Blue Lake—they are uniformly sized and spaced apart. Sites closest to the highway may have some road noise (sites 37, 80, 82 and 85 in particular). Some sites are closer to the beach: 1, 2, 20, 21, 55, 52, 53, 62 to 66 and 71, 1e and 11e. As is typical of boreal forest, the dense evergreen canopy does not permit enough light to reach the forest floor to permit much undergrowth to flourish. As a result, the campsites at Blue Lake are very open to each other and lacking in privacy. This is made up for in part by their spaciousness and by the quiet, family atmosphere of the park. Visitors will also want to know that Blue Lake is perhaps the best-maintained and cleanest campground in Northern Ontario.

Local Attractions

Blue Lake is not well situated for daytrips, and most campers here are quite content to confine their holiday to the park. Kenora has two-hour, narrated cruises of pretty Lake of the Woods aboard the M.S. *Kenora*. Dining is available. Also in Kenora, Abitibi Consolidated hosts tours of their massive paper plant weekdays during the summer. Visitors observe first-hand the process of turning raw timber into fine paper. (See Rushing River Provincial Park.) Those campers seeking a more active outdoors experience may wish to travel farther southwest to Rushing River Provincial Park and enjoy Mother Nature's riverside waterpark. It's a distinct change in atmosphere from placid Blue Lake.

Fast Facts

Campground: 198 sites in one campground (98 with hydro hookups); some sites wheelchair accessible; 3 backcountry sites. Group camping; 16-person staff house available during the winter. Comfort stations with flush toilets, showers, laundry (wheelchair accessible). Camping season mid-May to mid-September. Reservations recommended for all sites from early July to mid-August.

Supplies: Firewood sold in the park. Ice and groceries available just outside the park. Complete shopping in Vermilion Bay (8 km).

Facilities:
Trailer sanitation station
Seasonal storage of boats/trailers
Boat launch but no docking
Beach
Playground
Canoe rentals
Interpretive centre
Hiking trails (four trails totalling 15 km; one trail is barrier free)

Winter Use: The park has groomed cross-country and snowmobile trails.

Contact Information: Box 730, Dryden ON, P8N 2Z4 tel 807-227-2601

Caliper Lake Provincial Park

Location: On Highway 71 between Fort Frances and Kenora.
Natural Environment: 1   **Activities: 1**   **Campground: 2**

Caliper Lake is custom-made for a quiet family holiday. In fact, few parks in the province have such a luxuriously relaxed atmosphere. The main purpose of a visit here is to bask in northern beauty and serenity—the sheen of water under moonlight, the sweet pine fragrance, the wingbeat of an osprey. Although small in area (only 100 ha), the park has excellent birdwatching opportunities, and the majestic pines provide good shelter for campers. Caliper Lake is a calm lake, making it ideal for safe boating, canoeing, swimming and fishing.

Natural Environment and History

Tiny Caliper Lake is located just southeast of Lake of the Woods and is part of the same northern deciduous-evergreen forest zone as its better-known neighbour. The park's character comes from a verdant forest of huge red and white pine that thrive in the rich, glacier-deposited soil. Other northern trees found here include aspen, cedar, spruce and balsam fir.

The forest provides habitat for many small mammals, and deer are commonly seen along park trails. Caliper Lake is best known for its birdwatching opportunities. Grouse can often be spotted scurrying into the bush, eagles and osprey soar over the lake, and loons are commonly sighted on the lake, especially during the early morning or at night. Most interesting perhaps are the white pelicans—a highlight of any visit to Northwestern Ontario—and a surprise to many visitors. White pelicans extended their habitat from Lake of the Woods to Caliper Lake during the 1980s, and they are often seen feeding on the lake. Another exciting find for birdwatchers is the barred owl, which nests in the park. This northern bird is attracted by Caliper's quietness and does not usually breed in surrounding parks because of disturbing activity and noise levels.

Special Activities

Caliper Lake's size prohibits the operation of any regular interpretive programs. However, the presence of breeding barred owls allows for twice-weekly owl prowls presented by a visiting owl expert. After viewing an evening film, a talk and exhibits on owls at the outdoor amphitheatre, visitors are invited for a short hike (dogs not invited). Tape recordings of the barred owl's calls (which sound rather like monkeys chattering) are played and, invariably, barred owls fly in for a close-at-hand visit with fortunate campers. What a treat it is to see these magnificent birds in the pine boughs overhead—very close, in full voice, and often in family groups. Few camping experiences can top this one.

The lack of a regular schedule of events adds to rather than diminishes Caliper's appeal, because it's the lack of busy-ness that allows the charm of northern forest and lake to work its rejuvenating effect. Short hikes are available along a 2.5-km trail.

Most activity in the park takes place at the waterfront. A small but excellent sand beach provides warm swimming. This is one of the few parks that has a floating platform—excellent for shallow dives and much tomfoolery—increasing the play value of the beach many times over. The boat launch provides access to the lake for cruising or fishing for pike, pickerel and smallmouth bass. Canoeists tend to travel the shoreline in hopes of seeing wildlife. Longer-distance canoe trips may be taken along Caliper Lake and the Log River. Recreational equipment includes a beachside playground and picnic area. Canoes can be rented from the beach area.

Campground

Caliper Lake has 83 campsites and 26 of these have electrical hookups. Most campsites are under the shelter of large pines that provide a soft, deep carpet of needles underfoot. However, most of the sites are very open (pines provide too deep a shade for undergrowth) and are closely spaced, so there is little visual privacy. Sites with the greatest privacy are numbers 55, 56, 60 and 61. These are on the main camp road, which in a large park would be unpleasantly busy, but is just fine in quiet Caliper; the paved road is actually wonderfully free of dust. Excellent sites near the beach are numbers 28 and 29. The campground comfort station has toilets and showers but no laundry.

Local Attractions

The largest community close to Caliper Lake is Fort Frances. The Fort is the home of the Stone-Consolidated Corp., and guided tours of the plant are available to visitors over 12 years of age on weekdays during July and August. Machines as large as a football field roll out paper, and the entire trees-to-product process is explained. Additional tours by bus visit the corporate forest. Fort Frances also has a historic museum with displays on aboriginal artifacts, the fur trade, logging and farming.

Fast Facts

Campground: 83 sites (26 sites with hydro hookups); some sites wheelchair accessible. Group camping. Seasonal leasing. Comfort station with showers and flush toilets (wheelchair accessible). Camping season mid-May to mid-September. No reservations.

Supplies: Firewood and ice sold in the park. Some supplies available in Nestor Falls (7 km). Best shopping in Fort Frances (about 50 km).

Facilities:
Trailer sanitation station
Trailer/boat storage
Boat launches and docking
Beach
Playground
Hiking trails (one 2.5-km trail)

Winter Use: The park is closed in winter.

Contact Information: Box 188, Nestor Falls ON, P0X 1K0
tel 807-484-2181

Rushing River Provincial Park

Location: 20 km southeast of Kenora on Highway 71.

Natural Environment: 1   **Activities:** 2   **Campground:** 2

In Rushing River Provincial Park, Mother Nature provides a wonderful outdoor playground, a favourite destination of families from Northwestern Ontario and Manitoba. Rushing River tumbles over, under and between water-smoothed boulders, pausing occasionally in sun-warmed pools before continuing on its headlong rush. Youngsters (and their parents) slip, slide and clamber their way from pool to pool. The summertime delights of Rushing River don't stop at the river. Dogtooth Lake is a premier swimming hole, with three beach areas and the preferred sunning spot for teens, a small island that is easily reached by wading and swimming. Park staff are kept hopping all summer with a program for the entire family that includes guided hikes, movies, games and contests.

Natural Environment and History

The physical setting of Rushing River is typical of Ontario's north, where glaciers scoured bedrock through several ice ages and left behind an austere but beautiful landscape of lakes and rivers set within granite bedrock.

A noteworthy distinction of Rushing River Provincial Park is that these lands were the scene of a forest fire in 1910. Fire is a friend to jack pine, a tree that requires intense heat for its cones to open and release seed. Thus, the forest canopy here is handsome jack pine of uniform age—90 years. Over the decades, aspen and fir have taken hold, but jack pine predominates and determines the character of the park's scenery.

Rushing River is good wildlife habitat, though the busy nature of the campground area means that the best viewing is away from camp or in the off-season. Deer, bear, moose and mink are occasionally sighted here, in addition to beaver and otter. More commonly seen are birds, especially those species attracted to water, particularly loons, ducks, kingfishers and heron.

Special Activities

Rushing River is a very active park, with campers and day-use visitors participating in a vivid kaleidoscope of outdoors fun. Most people head for the waterfront. Dogtooth Lake has three beaches, and the delightful rapids of the river provide plenty of waterplay opportunities. The park rents paddleboats, kayaks and water trikes for enjoying the lake and river. Canoes may be rented at outfitters located very close to the park.

Canoeists paddle out into Dogtooth Lake to explore the pretty islands and inlets. From Dogtooth Lake, a short portage provides access to long-distance canoe adventures on Lake of the Woods, Gale Lake or Tilvert Lake. Park staff can provide printed guides and maps for all three canoe routes accessible from the park. Boaters make use of launches and a dock located in the campground; rentals are available from nearby outfitters or you can bring your own boat. Dogtooth Lake is fishing country for those seeking pickerel, pike, bass and lake trout.

This park has two short hiking trails suitable for family outings. The Beaver Pond Trail (1.5 km) takes walkers past a lily-speckled beaver pond, an excellent place to observe the comings and goings of kingfishers, turtles, herons and dragonflies. The Lower Rapids Trail (2 km) follows the Rushing River rapids and waterfalls, and has good picnic and photo spots. The Stokes Lake Trail (5 km) is a rather wet trail that is currently under improvement; the trail leads through a variety of forest types. On the trails and in the campground, visitors love to pick the many seasonal edibles provided by the forest—raspberries, blueberries, cherries and hazelnuts.

In the central campground area is the Loon's Nest, the park's interpretive centre, with displays on park wildlife and plants. Naturalists organize events all season long and have something happening each morning, afternoon and evening. Typical events include games, arts and crafts, slide shows and movies, instructional classes (for example, on how to use a compass), and evening spirit hikes.

Campground

Rushing River has 220 campsites (69 with hydro) in two campgrounds. Sites 1 to 38 (all hydro) are close to the interpretive centre, store, playground and the busiest beach. The sites here are very open and completely lacking in privacy. Sites 39 to 115 are more conventional sites on the south side of Dogtooth Lake. These sites are close to the Beaver Pond Trail, two beaches, the volleyball court and a boat launch. The spacing and openness of the sites means that the atmosphere is rather noisy and kinetic.

If privacy and quiet are more to your liking, then head for sites 200 to 278, located on the north side of Dogtooth Lake. These sites have their own playground, boat launch and beach, though they are a fair hike from the amphitheatre, interpretive centre and other busy locations. The sites on the water are excellent; many of these are suitable for tents only. The most recommended sites are 201 and 223 to 233.

Local Attractions

Rushing River Provincial Park is about 20 km southeast of Kenora, a convenient distance for a day of sightseeing and replenishing the campsite larder. The M.S. *Kenora* plies the waters of beautiful Lake of the Woods. Passengers enjoy two-hour narrated tours during the afternoons and evenings. Every cruise has dining, and on Sundays of long weekends a dance cruise takes place. Highlights of the cruise include cottages of the rich and famous, the Keewatin Boat Lift (which carries pleasure craft between Lake of the Woods and the Winnipeg River), and tall tales and legends of the region.

When in town, take the time to wander around and see the numerous murals that bedeck buildings in the downtown area. Over a dozen murals depict Kenora's history. More history is on display at the Lake of the Woods Museum. Changing exhibits chronicle Kenora's history from Hudson's Bay fur-trading fort to a tourism and paper-mill town.

Abitibi Consolidated offers public tours on summer weekdays. Four days a week, visitors tour the paper plant to watch trees become paper. Tours of the forestry operation take place weekly during the summer. Transportation to the forest is provided, as is lunch and other refreshments.

Lake of the Woods is excellent for fishing, boating, kayaking and canoeing. Outfitters in Kenora can supply all the rentals and lessons necessary, and can also arrange for eco-tours of nearby wilderness areas.

Fast Facts

Campgrounds: 191 sites in two campgrounds (38 sites with hydro hookups); one site wheelchair accessible. Group camping. Two tent trailers available for rent. Comfort stations with showers and flush toilets (wheelchair accessible). Camping season mid-May to late September. Reservations recommended for waterfront and hydro sites from late June to mid-August.

Supplies: Firewood sold in park. Grocery shopping and ice about 0.5 km from the park entrance. Best shopping in Kenora (20 km).

Facilities:
Trailer sanitation station
Trailers/boat storage
Boat launches and docking
Kayak, paddleboat and water-tricycle rentals
Canoe rentals just outside park
Beaches
Playground
Sports fields
Interpretive centre
Hiking trails (three trails totalling 8.5 km)

Winter Use: The park has one 3-kilometre ski trail.

Contact Information: Box 5160, Kenora ON, P9N 3X9
tel 807-548-4351

Quetico Provincial Park

Location: 130 km west of Thunder Bay off Highway 11.
Natural Environment: 3   Activities: 3   Campground: 1

Quetico's name summons up the sounds of the call of loons, the rustle of pine boughs and the drip of water from a glistening paddle. It is long-distance canoe tripping—and the possibility of exploring lakes seen by few other travellers—that calls campers to this border-straddling wilderness. Fortunately the park also provides a range of amenities enjoyed by the less intrepid, such as daylong canoe trips and hikes that lead to quiet lakes and old-growth forest. While the modest level of facilities and activities in the campground would be disappointing in another environment, the peaceful ambience of Quetico's campground is both appropriate and appreciated.

Natural Environment and History

Quetico is huge—over 475,000 hectares of serene lakes and rivers, seemingly untouched by human hand and awaiting discovery. Although the forest is largely northern in character, with such trees as spruce, jack pine, aspen and birch, southern hardwoods thrive where deeper soils and warmer temperatures permit. Thus, autumn in Quetico is lively with the colour provided by oak, maple and basswood. Isolated stands of huge, ancient red and white pine exist in the park—rare examples of trees that were not taken by loggers. Underneath the canopy of trees, and in any forest opening, a myriad of wildflowers provide grace and fragrance.

Quetico is fabulous for wildlife viewing, and a chance encounter with a moose or a bald eagle may well be a lasting memory of your camping trip. Otter, beaver, marten and mink are frequently seen, as are many smaller mammals. The park is also good for birdwatching. Colourful woodland warblers flit in the trees, the mellifluous call of the Swainson's thrush accompanies every hiker, and soaring bald eagle and osprey are mirrored in the surface of still lakes.

Quetico's awe-inspiring beauty is not a recent discovery. Archaeological evidence taken from pottery and pictographs suggests that hunters and fishermen visited here as early as 9,000 years ago. Later, the lakes and rivers were a highway for fur-traders and explorers heading to the western frontier. Logging was the primary industry here until recent times.

Special Activities

First and foremost, Quetico is a park for canoeists, with enough combinations of waterways, routes, distances and seasons to provide for a lifetime of backwoods serenity. Quetico has six access points for canoe trips, and each entry point has a ranger station that supplies maps and camping permits for the 2,200 wilderness campsites scattered across the park's interior. Local outfitters can provide any equipment or supplies necessary, and park staff can offer the experienced advice critical to planning a successful backcountry trip.

Visitors wanting a more traditional drive-in camping experience will find their needs met at the Dawson Trail Campground just off the Trans-Canada Highway. Seven hiking trails are accessed from the campground. Beaver Meadows Trail (2.5 km) takes hikers through a dazzling variety of habitat types, from wetlands to steep slopes. The French Falls Trail, a 2.4-km roundtrip, is not long, but it is surprisingly strenuous because of the steep topography en route. The path follows the cascades of the French River, which are very picturesque and offer great photo opportunities. The 0.8-km Pickerel Point Trail is the best option for lovers of marshland and their weird residents—frogs, heron, turtles and kingfishers. The Whiskey Jack Trail is a 2.5-km loop through wetlands and has some boardwalk sections. Visitors are introduced to bunchberry, sphagnum moss, twinflower, horsetail and other fascinating plants.

The Pines Hiking Trail (10 km) is very different from the other trails because it traverses areas of sandy soil (and not rock); the highlight of Pines is the chance to explore a grand old-growth pine forest. This is an extension of the Whiskey Jack Trail. The French Portage Trail (5 km) follows in the footsteps of voyageurs along the main route settlers trod on their trek to the Red River area of Manitoba. Even though Quetico is a wilderness park, it does have a wheelchair-accessible trail, the Pickerel River Trail. This is a 1.6-km trip through spruce forest lowlands and pine forested hills.

The interpretive program at the park has events almost daily during the summer. Instead of games and entertainment, the focus is on education through guided hikes, films, campfires, and programs on wilderness skills for kids. The wonderful visitor centre and library is a storehouse of information on the park environment, from easy-to-use trail guides and how-to canoe-trip books to academic studies of everything from forest fires to bald eagles. In addition to books, the library has videos, slides and photographs.

Quetico is no longer strictly a summer holiday spot. During the winter, visitors come to cross-country ski, snowshoe, ice fish and winter camp. Snowmobiling, like motorboating, is prohibited.

Campground

The only drive-in camping in the park is at the Dawson Trail. Two camp-grounds have a total of 107 sites (49 electrical). Both campgrounds have comfort stations with showers, flush toilets and laundries. The sites are under the protection of tall jack pines, which provide sweetly scented air and soft cover underfoot but provide poor visual privacy. Although this would detract considerably from the camp experience in most parks, campers at Quetico are usually so caught up in enjoying nature in quiet ways that campground noise is not often a difficulty.

The Chippewa Campground on French Lake has some well-spaced sites, particularly numbers 13, 14, 16, 18, 20 and 21; electrical sites 9e and 11e are also recommended. The Ojibwa Campground is the larger campground. It has two beaches on French Lake, although more sites overlook wetlands along Baptism Creek. The best sites are numbers 50 to 62 and 90, 92, 94, 95 and 100.

Local Attractions

Quetico is remote from most large communities. Visitors to the park spend their entire stay enjoying remarkable natural beauty and generally do not leave the park for daytrips to the surrounding region.

Fast Facts

Campgrounds: 104 sites in two campgrounds (49 sites with hydro hookups); some sites wheelchair accessible; 2,200 backcountry sites. Seasonal leasing. Comfort stations with showers and flush toilets (wheelchair accessible). Camping season from mid-May to mid-October. Reservations recommended for electrical sites all the time and for all sites on long weekends.

Supplies Firewood sold in park. Shopping available in Atikokan (45 km).

Facilities:
Trailer sanitation station
Canoe launches
Canoe rentals outside the park
Beaches
Interpretive centre
Hiking trails (seven trails totalling 26 km; one trail wheelchair accessible)

Winter Use: The park is open to skiers all winter, but no park services are provided.

Contact Information: Atikokan ON, P0T 1C0 tel 807-597-4602

Kakabeka Falls Provincial Park

Location: 32 km west of Thunder Bay on Highway 11/17.
Natural Environment: 2   **Activities: 1**   **Campground: 1**

Fabulous Kakabeka Falls, a 39-m curtain of white water cascading over a slate precipice, struck awe into everyone who passed this way, from aboriginal inhabitants to early explorers. This small, 420-ha park encompasses the falls and the gorge downstream, including the very paths fur-traders trod while portaging around the falls. Kakabeka Falls is worth a visit for a day or two of swimming and hiking, and the park is also a superb base for exploring the region's many attractions.

Natural Environment and History

Kakabeka Falls Provincial Park is a rewarding destination for anyone with an interest in geology. The history of this site goes way back, and fossils found in the layers of ancient volcanic rock that make up the fall's ledges have been dated at 1.6-billion years. More recent, in geologic terms, is the work of the glaciers during the last ice age, about 10,000 years ago. Glacial meltwaters carved out the precipitous gorge of the Kaministiquia River and created a large river delta upon which the campgrounds are situated. Geologists note that although grey sedimentary rock underlays much of the park, the north end of the park is pink granite. Thus the park is a contact point between rock types.

The forest along the river is a mixture of deciduous and coniferous species. Pine, hemlock, birch and maple grow particularly vigorously here, perhaps aided by the extra humidity from the fine river-spray that usually hangs in the air. Because the region is a mix of northern and southern forest types, the park protects some locally rare plants species such as bur oak. The landscape is diversified by the open meadows and shallow ponds created by beaver dams. Other animals that inhabit Kakabeka include bear, deer, painted turtle and an abundance of small mammals.

Kakabeka Falls not only celebrates a natural wonder, but also protects the memory of important human history. To the region's original inhabitants, the falls were known as Kakabeka, or "steep cliffs." The fall's reputation spread more widely after the first explorers and missionaries walked the river's edge, and they became an important landmark on the route of Fort William's fur traders. By 1904, the falls were less important as a navigational impediment than as a source of power, and a hydroelectric dam was built here.

Special Activities

Kakabeka Falls is known for its pleasant riverside hiking trails. Visitors return again and again to walk in the pathways of the voyageurs. Six trails vary in length and difficulty. Poplar Point Trail (3.6 km) winds through the campground area and is an easy walk, suitable for young children. The 5.6-km-long Beaver Meadows Trail is one of the more interesting walks; its route incorporates the remains of an old farm, a beaver pond and meadow, a glacial spillway and some scenic views of the river. An extension to Beaver Meadows is the River Terrace Loop (3.6 km), which also has good river views. The Contact Trail (one kilometre) meanders along the river upstream of the falls, near the beach and swimming area. Little Falls Trail (3 km) is more rugged than the other trails, and has outstanding views of the river. The trail descends into the river valley depths to the Little Falls and leads you on an invigorating ascent out of the gorge.

Mountain Portage Trail (one-kilometre loop) is wheelchair accessible and is perhaps the most popular trail in the park. This is the exact route that voyageurs and missionaries, natives and armies took to walk around the falls. Mountain Portage includes walkways along the very edge of the cliffs near the falls, where it the air is often wet with mist. The overlooks that extend over the cliff rim provide photographers with excellent vantage points of the falls and gorge.

Although waterfalls and hydro dams make for currents too dangerous for swimming, upstream from the falls is a beach and marked swimming area.

Planned activities at Kakabeka Falls include guided hikes, children's programs and campfires. Other regularly scheduled activities include daylong hikes, a weekend to celebrate voyageurs, and a duck race.

Kakabeka Falls is one of the most-photographed winter scenes in the province, the falls an ever-changing sculpture of water and ice, the frozen mist turning the nearby trees into sparkling statues. The park is a popular daytrip for cross-country skiing. Thirteen kilometres of trails are groomed, and they are suitable for all skiers, beginners to experts, for both classic and skate-style skiing.

Campground

The park has three campgrounds with 169 spacious campsites; 79 of these sites have electricity. Comfort stations with flush toilets, showers and laundries are located in each campground. Riverside Campground (sites 200 to 230) and Fern's Edge Campground (sites 231 to 274) are closest to the falls, and also closest to the highway, so noise may be a factor to consider here. The best sites are Fern's Edge numbers 231, 260 and 274. All electric sites are located in the Whispering Hills Campground (sites 1 to 94); this campground has many pull-through sites for large trailers.

Local Attractions

Continue your step back through time at fabulous old Fort William, an extraordinary journey to a palisaded fur-trading community on the northwest frontier. Costumed interpreters—equipped with expert knowledge and a good measure of gusto—take on roles as voyageurs, traders, doctors, farmers and military men. Daily events include cannon and musket drills, freighter canoe rides, wagon rides, a gentleman's tea, song and dance celebrations, trades demonstrations, freighter canoe arrivals, and much more. The dozens of buildings include trader's houses, an apothecary, the Great Hall (dining room for North West Company partners), houses, and a working farm. On Wednesdays in July and August, the Fort invites you to partake of a voyageur feast, complete with entertainment and stories. On other days, the cafeteria supplies modern versions of period dishes such as pea soup, freshly baked bread and berry crisps.

Fast Facts

Campgrounds: 160 sites in three campgrounds (90 sites with hydro hookups); some sites are wheelchair accessible. Group camping. Seasonal leasing. Comfort stations with showers, laundry, flush toilets (wheelchair accessible). Camping season from mid-May to mid-October. Reservations recommended for hydro sites all season.

Supplies: Firewood sold in the park. Supplies available in the village of Kakabeka Falls (one kilometre).

Facilities:
Trailer sanitation station
Beach
Playground
Hiking trails (six trails totalling 14 km)

Winter Use: The park has 25 to 30 km of groomed cross-country trails.

Contact Information: 435 James St. S. Suite 221, Thunder Bay ON, P7E 6S8 tel 807-473-9231

Sleeping Giant Provincial Park

Location: 83 km east of Thunder Bay, 42 km south of
    Highway 17 on Highway 587.
Natural Environment: 3   Activities: 3   Campground: 1

Sleeping Giant Provincial Park (formerly Sibley) is a must-see among Ontario's parks. Exceptional hiking, sea kayaking and warm-water swimming are attractive to campers and daytrippers alike. Hiking trails travel to towering iron-red cliffs, numerous lakes and secluded coastal coves. Picturesque Silver Islet (located just outside park boundaries) was once a rich mining town and, though it is now a cottage community, retains its frontier charm. Sleeping Giant is popular for family gatherings all summer long, and its densely packed campground can be rather busy. The lack of solitude at your campsite, however, is a small price to pay for all that the park has to offer.

Natural Environment and History

Sleeping Giant is located on a narrow peninsula that juts south into Lake Superior. The park is huge—over 24,000 ha—and the developed campground area is at the south end of the peninsula. Viewed from a distance, the peninsula's profile strikingly resembles a reclining human figure, hence the park's name. The oldest rock on the peninsula dates back 1.7 billion years, and the differing layers of rock built upon the sedimentary base are exposed as layers in dramatic cliffs; these are the highest vertical cliffs in the province. Weirdly shaped rock outcrops along the wild Superior shore, such as the arch known as the Sea Lion, are hard diabase—molten rock that seeped up from the subsurface of the earth.

Sleeping Giant has over 20 distinct habitat types. The park was created to protect the last white and red pine stands on the Sibley Peninsula from being completely eradicated by lumbering. Although this forest is mainly aspen, birch and balsam fir, there are also stands of cedar and black spruce in low-lying locations. Sleeping Giant is best known for two plant groups, orchids and ferns. The 30 species of orchid found here include Ontairo's rarest: bog adder's-mouth and small round-leaved orchis. About 38 species of fern thrive in the damp conditions on the cliffs and talus slopes in the southern part of the park. Other habitats rewarding for botanists on the prowl are small areas of subarctic plants on exposed, harsh coastal areas or on the windy heights of the Giant's crags.

Sleeping Giant is excellent for wildlife viewing, and many visitors see white-tailed deer and smaller mammals such as racoon, skunk, beaver, fisher and marten. Wolves inhabit the park and their howls are occasionally heard in remoter areas. At least 75 bird species breed in the park, and migrants and visitors swell the park checklist to 200 species. Northern birds such as the black-backed three-toed woodpecker are found in the same vicinity as southern birds such as parula warbler.

Special Activities

Sleeping Giant is a hiker's delight. All adventurers should pick up the trail guide available at the visitor centre. Eight nature trails (0.5 to 2.4 km in length) are short, easy walks. Several trails have interpretive signs that provide information on wildlife, plants, geology and park ecology. Plantain Lane is especially well suited to wheelchairs.

Long-distance hiking is provided on 11 interior trails—all of which are rewarding for day hikes or overnight trips. The longest and most popular is the Kabeyun Trail (40 km), which runs along the western shore of the park and provides access to the remarkable cliff-face of the Giant. Other trails introduce visitors to unusual ecosystems: old-growth pines (Pickerel Lake); wet fens (Middlebrun Bay); and a diabase dyke (the Sea Lion—a coastal rock formation). Wildlife viewing is very good along Burma Trail and Talus Lake Trail. Many of these trails provide spectacular views of the Giant, interior lakes, and secluded coves where waves pound and froth over rock formations and pebble beaches.

A visit to Sleeping Giant is not complete without a walk up and along the Sleeping Giant itself. One approach is to mountain bike, or hike, from the Kabeyun South Trail Head to a point near Lehtinen's Bay where the trail becomes too steep for biking. Bikes may be left locked at this point, and the ascent continued on foot through the narrow, steep cavern called the Chimney, up to the Giant's "knees." The intrepid are rewarded with a view that takes in Thunder Bay, Isle Royale, and Silver Islet. This trip should not be attempted when conditions are wet because the very steep slopes of talus (rock and pebble eroded from the upper heights) become treacherously slippery. An easier but still steep climb accesses the Giant's chest by way of the Sawyer Bay Trail (a route known for good berry-picking). The views at the chest take in lovely Sawyer Bay and the rolling hills north of Highway 17.

Visitors unable to take in an athletic hike can still enjoy breathtaking panoramas from Thunder Bay Lookout at the north end of the Kabeyun Trail (a rough road leads in to a parking lot at the lookout). Visitors cautiously step out onto a wooden viewing platform and gasp at the view: 100 m below their feet the pine and birch sway in the wind; birds of prey soar past; and aquamarine Lake Superior stretches to Thunder Bay on the horizon.

One of the delights of Sleeping Giant is the beautiful visitor centre, maintained by the Friends of Sleeping Giant. Displays describe park geology, plants, animals, and the history of Silver Islet. Volunteers lead hikes, organize group campfires and games, perform skits, and present movies. The diverse program, presented at the centre, at an outdoor amphitheatre and on a beachside stage, includes topics such as sled dogs, backwoods survival and aboriginal legends.

Campground

Marie Louise Campground has 190 campsites (64 electrical). Because the campsites are average to small in size, and are located close together, Sleeping Giant is not for those who want a quiet camping experience. The best odds for a quieter site are numbers 121 to 140 (some with their own trail to the beach); and numbers 104 to 115 (also some with private waterfront access). The park has 20 interior sites for hikers, and these should be reserved well in advance. The campground has a long sandy beach on Marie Louise Lake. A group campground accommodates up to 100 people.

Local Attractions

Silver Islet, a quaint community considered one of Ontario's best-preserved ghost towns, will delight photographers with historic charm and a harbour sheltered by green islands. Although Silver Islet was once the richest silver mine in the world, its miner's cottages are now summer cottages, little changed in style and surroundings. The original town store still stands at the centre of the village; it is a good source for cottage supplies and books and serves excellent afternoon teas. It's well worth a visit to the village just to examine the exquisite historic photographs on the store walls of Silver Islet and its early inhabitants. Silver Islet has several streets, each equally enjoyable for walking; residents can point out the town jail and other points of interest.

The Thunder Bay region is renowned for amethysts, and rock hounds can visit several mines in the area that invite visitors to find their own sparkling purple souvenir. Visitors dig through dirt and boulders with hands and trowels to find their gems, and the finding is very easy. Cost is calculated per pound, and rock shops with finished gems and jewellery provide labour-free souvenirs. Ask at the Sleeping Giant Visitor Centre or at the park gate for the closest mines.

Ouimet Canyon Provincial Park is a day-use facility created to preserve a magnificent wilderness canyon that is a photographer's delight. The park is accessed by way of a sideroad north of Highway 17 approximately 30 km east of Highway 587 (the road leading south to Sleeping Giant). A sign indicates the turn-off from Highway 17, although the sign occasionally disappears at the hands of vandals. Ouimet has several trails with viewing platforms; interpretive displays describe the unique park environment. Plants and animals normally found hundreds of kilometres to the north survive in the chilly subarctic conditions in the canyon.

Fast Facts

Campground: 190 sites in one campground (64 sites with hydro hookups); some sites wheelchair accessible; 40 backcountry sites. Group camping. Seasonal leasing. Comfort stations with showers, laundry, flush toilets (wheelchair accessible). Camping season mid-May to mid-October. Reservations recommended for all sites all summer long.

Supplies: Firewood and ice sold in park. Basic needs can be met at Silver Islet (5km) or Pass Lake (20 km). Complete shopping is a long way away, so purchase supplies before entering park.

Facilities:
Trailer sanitation station
Trailers/boat storage
Boat launch and docking
Canoe and boat rentals
Beach
Playground
Hiking trails (11 trails totalling 64 km, some trails are wheelchair accessible)

Winter Use: The park is open all winter and has extensive cross-country ski trails (30 km). Sleeping Giant's cross-country competitions attract hundreds of participants from all over.

Contact Information: General Delivery, Pass Lake ON, P0T 2M0
tel 807-977-2526

Rainbow Falls Provincial Park

Location: About 15 km west of Terrace Bay on Highway 17.
Rossport Campground is on the shore of Lake Superior;
Rainbow Falls is about 5 km east.
Natural Environment: 2 **Activities:** 1 **Campground:** 1

"Canyon Country" is the grand moniker given the wild country that lies between Lake Superior and Lake Nipigon. The region is noted for its steep hills, excellent hiking and cross-country skiing. Rainbow Falls Provincial Park is a park in two parts. Campers who want their tent to billow with sea breezes head for the campground on the Lake Superior shore. On the north side of the Trans-Canada Highway, the wooded hills around Whitesand Lake provide good cycling and hiking, and the campground has a beach and a playground. The Whitesand River descends a steep gorge within the park, bubbling and foaming over granite boulders and fallen trees en route. A convenient boardwalk descends the gorge alongside the river, and is a delight to both campers and travellers who visit the park for a picnic.

Natural Environment and History

The two main sections of Rainbow Falls Provincial Park are dramatically different in character. The Rossport Campground section is quite flat, a mere crescent of shoreline from which to observe Superior's vast blueness. The larger portion of the park is 5 km away in the Whitesand Lake Campground, which at first glance seems typical of Northern Ontario—ever-present granite, forested hills, a quiet lake. It's only when visitors descend the stairs alongside the Whitesand River that they realize Mother Nature worked a little harder on this locale. The river cascades over dozens of rocky ledges, its erratic course following crevices in the bedrock. The rock glistens in a dozen brilliant hues, the colours highlighted by splashes of whitewater. When the sun shines through the river mists, rainbows can be observed in several places at once. The high concentration of white birch, the colourful rocks and the river form a picture-perfect backdrop for photos.

The trees do not grow as large or as luxuriantly at Rainbow Falls as elsewhere because of the thin soils that remained after a forest fire during the 1800s. Smaller plants include bog cranberry, Labrador tea, blueberry, bluebead lily, and blue flag iris. Wildlife present in the park is mainly small mammals such as squirrels, fox and chipmunks, though moose, lynx and bear are present occasionally. Avian life observed in the park includes loons, osprey, Canada goose, and peregrine falcon, as well as the ubiquitous chickadee.

Special Activities

With such pretty surroundings, it's no wonder that most campers head for the trails. The 3-kilometre Rainbow Falls Trail is the most popular. Not actually a trail, it is a series of stairs and observation platforms that follow the pretty falls along their 60-m descent. The trail then leaves the river to ascend to a lookout over both Whitesand Lake and Lake Superior. The Superior Trail is a rocky 2.4-km path to yet another lookout over Lake Superior.

Hikers speak enthusiastically about the Voyageur Hiking Trail, a 50-km trek through the "canyon country" from Terrace Bay to Rossport; it combines great scenery, solitude and strenuous exercise. The Voyageur Trail passes through the park for about 3 km. Many people follow the Rainbow Falls Trail to its end and then continue their hike along the Voyageur to Rossport.

There's plenty of good family biking at Rainbow Falls. In addition to the park roads, there is the "Back 40 Road," which climbs to an excellent view of Whitesand Lake and is considered moderately difficult off-road biking (2.8 km).

Fisherfolk try their luck on both Whitesand Lake and Lake Superior. The former has pike and bass, and the latter is lake trout and whitefish territory.

The interpretive program at Rainbow Falls includes campfires, movies and slide shows, guest speakers, and special children's activities. Most activities take place on weekends. A cabin at the west beach in the Whitesand Lake Campground is the location of most programs.

The summer's highlight is the Canoe Regatta and Corn Roast held on the first weekend in August. The beach at Whitesand Lake is the scene of canoe races, children's contests and games, and a corn roast. It's always a popular weekend.

Campground

The Rossport Campground has 36 campsites, 16 of them with hydro hookups. These sites lack any privacy, but are large, open and flat—ideal for larger trailers and motorhomes. The lakeside sites, number 12, 15 to 21 and 24 and 25, have splendid views of Lake Superior. The campground has a comfort station but no laundry.

The Whitesand Lake Campground has 97 campsites (49 electrical) in five different areas. Some of the nicest, most private campsites in Ontario are in the Lakeside Campground (sites 66 to 70) high on a bluff. The electrical sites are in the Selim area, and many of these are long pull-throughs for trailers. The electrical sites, while close together, are not usually full and are thus quiet. All campsites in Whitesand Lake Campground have good access to the hiking trails, two beaches, a boat launch, dock, playground and picnic area.

Local Attractions

The village of Rossport, about 10 km from the Whitesand Lake Campground, is a delight. Unlike the lumber and mining towns on the rest of the Superior coast, Rossport is a bona fide fishing village. The town dock serves a small commercial fishery as well as the numerous pleasure cruisers that explore the coastline and islands. The main street is a very pleasant stroll, with fish restaurants, an inn and an art gallery. Rossport Island Tours is a cruise company that takes visitors on daytrips and longer adventures on a 40-ft cruiser equipped with all conveniences. Overnight and day cruises visit sheltered harbours and beaches for agate picking and bird-watching. Dinner cruises are available, as is a two-hour sightseeing excursion through the archipelago just offshore from Rossport.

Fast Facts

Campgrounds: Rossport Campground has 36 campsites (16 with hydro hookups); Whitesand Lake Campground has 97 campsites (49 with hydro hookups); some sites wheelchair accessible. Seasonal leasing. Comfort station with showers, laundry and flush toilets (wheelchair accessible). Camping season from mid-May to mid-September. Reservations recommended for hydro sites in July and August, all sites on weekends.

Supplies: Firewood and ice sold in park. Closest shopping is in Schreiber (about 10 km).

Facilities:
Trailer sanitation station
Boat launch but no docking
Bike and canoe rentals
Beaches
Playground
Bike trail (one trail totalling 2.8 km)
Hiking (three trails totalling about 7 km)
Boat launch

Winter Use: The park has 20 km of groomed cross-country ski trails for intermediate skiers.

Contact Information: Box 280, Terrace Bay ON, P0T 2W0
tel 807-824-2298

Neys Provincial Park

Location: 26 km west of Marathon, off Highway 17.
Natural Environment: 3   **Activities: 2**   **Campground: 2**

Lava flows…prisoners of war…logging camps…wild elk. When intriguing human history and remarkable environmental features converge, we often find the makings of an extraordinary park. And so it is at Neys Provincial Park, 3,440 hectares of wild shoreline and forest located in the northeastern corner of Lake Superior. Neys Provincial Park is a favourite for photographers—a memorable collage of ancient granite outcrops set in a very blue sea, colourful kayaks beached after a trip, the quiet boreal forest in the background. Neys has an excellent beach, good hiking trails, canoe and bike rentals and a visitor centre.

Natural Environment and History

Mother Nature used great imagination and powerful forces to forge the landscape called Neys. About one billion years ago, rock from within the Earth was forced up to the surface in concentric rings, and although glaciation removed many rock types from the peninsula, this hard bedrock stayed put to form the backbone of Neys. Through four different ice ages and eons of erosion, the rock is now softly twisted plaits of subdued grey—a sculpture in bedrock.

The park's cold and windy location on the exposed coast of Lake Superior means that the forest comprises tough species such as white spruce, fir, birch and aspen. Wetlands support black spruce, tamarack and cedar. Botanists come to Neys to study crowberry, encrusted saxifrage and other subarctic species.

Animals seen in the park include spruce grouse, osprey, moose, bear and deer. Neys was once the haunt of woodland caribou, but they have been chased off by railroad development, forest fires and hunting. A small group of caribou is sometimes seen along the shoreline, though not frequently; many more live on Pic and Slate Islands.

Archaeologists tell us that humans arrived here about 4,000 years ago. More recently, the local community of Coldwell was a thriving fishing village turned railroad town that was ultimately abandoned. During the Second World War the isolated Neys peninsula was a camp for German prisoners-of-war, famous for its lack of confinement since escapees would find themselves in thick bush or in cold Lake Superior.

Special Activities

The focus of most activity at Neys is on the shoreline, as this splendid 2-km beach is made for walking. In midsummer the water is just warm enough for wading, if you are a hardy sort, and the Little Pic River is also swimmable. Kids love the rock formations along the shore—they make sun-warmed and very smooth waterslides. Boaters take advantage of the boat launch to head out onto Lake Superior for fishing. Canoe rentals are available in the park, although canoeists are advised to stay close to shore since Superior is notoriously hazardous for paddlers.

Neys is a large park renowned for its spectacular beauty. The best plan for a stay at Neys is to use the four highly recommended hiking trails to find several good scenic overlooks. (The trails are also worthwhile for their educational value.) The Point Trail (one kilometre) follows the shore of Prisoner's Cove to Prisoner Point, a good spot for shoreline sunning, photographs and wading. Better yet, wade to the Prisoner Point from the beach, since the lake bottom is rippled sand and the water only shin-deep. From Prisoner Point, walk the 2-km Under the Volcano Trail, which is a must-see while you are in the park. Excellent signboards along the trail explain the volcanic and glacial forces that created the gnarled rock outcrops and boulder beaches that you stand on.

Two other trails, the Dune Trail (1.2 km) and the Lookout Trail (2 km) take hikers inland. The former explores the world of sand dune plants and animals while the second trail ascends a forested hill to a rocky ridge for a lookout over Lake Superior and Pic Island, a sight made famous by painter Lawren Harris.

The visitor centre has changing exhibits on the natural environment and history of the park. Most interesting is the model of the prisoner-of-war camp. Testimony from former guards and prisoners make for fascinating reading. Other displays document the many shipwrecks that lie just offshore. Naturalist-led events include guided hikes, movies, slide talks and guest speakers; these take place about three days a week during the summer. The highlight of the summer is Neys Nostalgia Days in mid-August, which include a spirit campfire, free bannock and pea-soup dinner, canoe races, native dancers and games.

Campground

There are 144 campsites in four separate areas with a central comfort station. Areas 1 to 3 are located along the shore, while Area 4 stretches inland and has some sites along the Little Pic River. Area 1 has pull-through electrical sites that are very open though convenient to the visitor centre; sites 25 and 26 are the best of these. Area 2 is the most recommended campground area, and the beachside sites are numbers 65 to 77. Area 3 has several nice electrical sites, especially those on the loop road farthest from the beach (sites numbered 28e to 44e). Area 4 has some of the most private sites, although noise from the CPR railway may be a nighttime problem for some campers. The best site in Area 4 may be site 99, which has a nice view of the Little Pic River and good access to the boat launch.

Local Attractions

Neys is located in a rather remote section of Lake Superior's shore. The nearest communities are Marathon and Terrace Bay. Both towns have restaurants and shops. Sixty kilometres to the west of the park is the truly delightful, photogenic village of Rossport. (See Rainbow Falls Provincial Park.)

Fast Facts

Campground: 144 sites in four campgrounds (61 sites with hydro hookups); some sites wheelchair accessible. Seasonal leasing. Comfort station with showers, flush toilets and laundry (wheelchair accessible). Camping season mid-May to mid-September. Reservations recommended for all sites for all weekends.

Supplies: Firewood sold in park. Many needs can be met at the store at the park entrance. Groceries available in Marathon (26 km).

Facilities:
Trailer sanitation station
Boat launch but no docking
Canoe and bike rentals
Interpretive centre (accessible)
Beach
Playground
Hiking (four trails totalling 5 km)

Contact Information: Box 280, Terrace Bay ON, P0T 2W0
tel 807-229-1624

Lake Nipigon Provincial Park

Location: 60 km north of Nipigon on Highway 11.
    About 160 km northeast of Thunder Bay.
Natural Environment: 2   Activities: 1   Campground: 2

Lake Nipigon has an impressive entryway: the route into the park is sandwiched between the sparkling surface of Lake Helen and looming, 170-m cliffs. And the park's stranger-than-life landscape remains true beyond its introduction. Lake Nipigon is the largest lake entirely within Ontario's borders—a wild inland sea of great depths, great cold and great fishing. Nipigon's beaches are of unearthly black sand, and many a trip to the park has been made just to see this unusual site. What is familiar in this landscape is the quality of the park experience. Smaller visitor numbers guarantee a tranquil atmosphere, and for boaters and fishers particularly, Lake Nipigon Provincial Park's 1,200 hectares are heaven sent.

Natural Environment and History

The cliffs that loom over your shoulder during your trip into the park are made of diabase that seeped up through the Earth's surface about one billion years ago. The diabase contains a green mineral, pyroxene, which was eroded into small sand grains and is now washed up by the waters of Lake Nipigon to form its landmark dark beaches.

Over time, the diabase created a soil environment suitable for typical boreal forest. Loggers removed much of the tree cover early in the 1900s, but spared some of the original spruce, red and jack pine, fir, poplar and cedar. Regenerating forest is largely composed of those pioneers of the north, white birch and trembling aspen. This park is well known for its luxuriant wildflower bloom from June through August.

The cliffs have another role to play in the landscape: they are lofty, protected habitat for the bald eagles and osprey that cruise the lake for fish. Lake Nipigon is also the home of another fish-eating bird, the double-crested cormorant. The lake has a healthy fish population, particularly of lake trout, which thrive in the deep and cold waters. Campers may also observe grouse, heron, snowshoe hare, beaver, deer and moose.

Special Activities

Boaters adore the wide-open spaces and uncrowded conditions of Lake Nipigon. The lake is notorious for windy conditions and frigid waters, though, so caution and experience are advised, particularly for canoeists. Fishing is by far the most common activity in the park, lake trout being the catch of choice. The world record for a speckled trout (7 kg) was set here at Lake Nipigon in 1916, and ever since, the lake has been a hotspot for anglers. Indeed, one of the world's most-used trout lures, the "muddler," was developed right here. A boat launch and dock are near the main park beach.

The beach is a must-see for its grey-black sands alone, and though the water never gets very warm, it is swimmable in midsummer. Because the park is so empty of visitors, several hours of beachcombing and quiet appreciation of the surrounding beauty can be deeply therapeutic.

Each of the three short trails in the park is described in an interpretive brochure. The Towering Aspen Trail (3 km) follows old logging roads. The Scenic Lookout Trail (2 km) begins at the main park beach (appropriately named Blacksand Beach) and ascends to a lookout with a wide-angle view of the bay, the very blue lake and several islands. Convenient rest stops are provided along the way. The Historic Site Trail (one kilometre) is a fascinating trip back in time; the trail visits the site of a Hudson's Bay post and an Indian settlement. The route passes a tiny, poignant cemetery with the graves of native and white settlers.

The park does not have an interpretive program. Instead, campers are encouraged to enjoy the lake and forest in their own way.

Campgrounds

Although this is a large park, the campground has only 60 sites. More than one visitor has exclaimed at how few campers there are and the possibility of having a premium campsite at any time in the season. Indeed, there are usually more excellent lakeside sites than there are campers to fill them. Many campsites have front-row seats for the splendid sunsets for which Lake Nipigon is renowned, and campers can watch a sailpast of ducks and loons from their front door. The best sites are 18, 28, 34 (28 and 34 have good beach access), 37, and 40 to 52 (even numbers only).

Twenty of the sixty sites are pull-throughs suitable for larger trailers. No sites have electricity. The comfort station has showers, flush toilets and a laundry.

Local Attractions

The town of Beardmore is 17 km north of the park. Once a gold mining boomtown, Beardmore is a convenient place to stock up on camp supplies. Just south of the park is the hamlet of Macdiarmid, where you can purchase fresh fish at a small commercial fishery. Farther south still is the breathtaking beauty of Lake Superior. The towns of Nipigon and Red Rock are active in promoting tourism in their "Canyon Country," and have worked hard to build trails for long-distance hiking and skiing in the region. Inquire in the towns for maps and other information on the trails.

Fast Facts

Campgrounds: 60 sites in one campground. Comfort station with showers, flush toilets and laundry (only toilets wheelchair accessible). Camping season early June to early September. Reservations usually not necessary.

Supplies: Firewood sold in park. Supplies available in Beardmore (17 km) and in Nipigon (about 60 km).

Facilities:
Trailer sanitation station
Boat launch and dock
Beach
Hiking trails (three trails totalling 6 km)

Winter Use: The park is closed in winter.

Contact Information: Box 970, Nipigon ON, P0T 2J0 tel 807-887-5000

Pukaswka National Park

Location: 25 km east of Marathon, off Highway 17 on the northeast coast of Lake Superior.

Natural Environment: 3   **Activities: 3**   **Campground: 3**

Pukaswka National Park is a park like no other in Ontario. It is simply the best place to revel in Lake Superior's splendour. Sea kayakers explore remote coves where turquoise breakers foam against boulders and beaches, and hikers test their mettle against the 60-km Coastal Trail with its infamous hanging bridge. Most of us, however, return to Pukaswka time and again for the remarkable tranquillity of the park, a palpable presence not only in the backcountry but in the campground as well. If you have a soul that can't live without wild places, then your holiday destination should be Pukaswka—one of Ontario's quietest parks, and perhaps its most beautiful.

Natural Environment and History

Lake Superior's immensity and coldness determine almost every aspect of life in the park. The wildly changeable maritime weather (fog to violent downpour to serene sunshine in a half day) can play havoc with plans for outdoor enjoyment. The lake—usually the water temperature is around 4°C—chills the forest and hills and limits the kinds of plants and animals that can survive here to only the very hardiest. The boreal forest is predominantly spruce, often stunted by the harsh climate and poor soils. Where the rock has eroded to produce slightly more productive soil, a mixed forest of cedar, fir, aspen and birch grows. In these areas the moist air encourages the growth of plentiful mosses underfoot. Exposed rocks are habitat for alpine and arctic plants normally found hundreds of kilometres farther north.

The animal life of Pukawska is typical of northern forest, and bear, moose and wolf inhabit the park. The park's most interesting creature is the woodland caribou, a species once plentiful in the province and now drastically reduced in number. These regal animals feed on the park's healthy population of lichens (200 species are reported to grow here). Parks literature and displays in the visitor centre explore the woodland caribou's remarkable adaptation to life in northern environments.

Proof of aboriginal use of the land is provided by the curious Pukaskwa Pits, depressions about two metres long and with stone walls one metre in height. It is believed these pits were created between 5,000 and 10,000 years ago, but their purpose is lost in time. Voyageurs, trappers, miners and loggers have all used the natural resources of the area, but none remained to form a permanent settlement.

Special Activities

Pukawska is a dream come true for outdoor adventurers, as the park has exceptional conditions for canoeing, kayaking and hiking. The park has three short trails. Halfway Lake Trail (2 km) forms a circuit around Halfway Lake and visits typical Canadian Shield scenery. The Southern Headland Trail travels through mixed forest to the Superior coastline and splendid views of water-dashed rock. Any hiker will want to spend a few hours marvelling at the power of Lake Superior and the lovely view of Pic Island. An extension of the Southern Headland Trail, the Beach Trail, leads through sheltered boreal forest, offering views of Pic River Dunes, the largest dune complex on Superior's north shore. Horseshoe Bay Trail provides access to a stunningly beautiful cove and beach. Even better than beachcombing is the chance to study the pond life in the pools of water that collect on the shoreline boulders.

Many hikers come to the park to travel the 60-km Coastal Trail that runs from the campground along the coast to the North Swallow River. Daytrips on the trail are also possible, the most popular being a 15-km hike from the campground to the White River crossing. This takes about five to seven hours and includes one of the trail's highlights, the suspension bridge over the White River. The bridge can be a challenge for those uncomfortable with swinging hundreds of metres over whitewater and waterfalls.

Pukaswka has two canoe routes. The entire White River Route runs 114 km and begins upstream from White Lake. A common shortcut is to begin at White Lake Provincial Park and paddle to Pukaswka. It is a five-day trip through forest and wetlands once travelled by natives and fur traders. The Coastal Canoe Route can be paddled by canoe or kayak, but a high level of experience and skill is required. This 180-km route runs all the way from Marathon just north of the park south to Michipicoten Harbour near Wawa, and takes 10 to 14 days to complete. Of course, many canoe daytrips can be made in the sheltered coves near the campground—and that is the best plan for any but the most experienced canoe trippers.

Hikers and canoeists must register for backcountry trips, and may make use of the 32 interior camping sites. These are deluxe sites with tent pads, firepits, outhouses and bear-proof receptacles. Park staff can supply the names and contact information for several local outfitters that will sell or rent equipment and supplies for canoeing and hiking. Boat chartering services and shuttle services for canoe trippers are provided by nearby outfitters.

Lake trout, salmon and whitefish are sought after on Lake Superior. Although there are fish populations in Pukaskwa's rivers and lakes, the populations are stressed from the difficult environment, and catch-and-release practices are encouraged.

The park's interpretive program includes the usual guided hikes, movies and illustrated talks, but also has two unique aspects. The first is the inclusion of significant First Nations content. The second is the degree of effort made to accommodate differing physical needs. Displays in the visitor centre come with cassette recordings for the visually impaired and closed captioning for the deaf. In addition, park visitors may make use of the park's all-terrain wheelchair.

Snowshoers and winter campers can enjoy the beauty of the north under a blanket of snow. There is one ungroomed cross-country ski trail. Snowmobiling is prohibited.

Campground

The campground has 67 sites (29 electrical). Three of these sites are secluded walk-in sites within the main campground. Although this is a remote, wilderness park, a high degree of wheelchair mobility is possible. Two campsites, all buildings and a boardwalk hiking trail to Hattie Cove are accessible. The campground is designed for maximum privacy, and quiet reigns throughout. The sites are equally attractive, but the most private are numbers 12, 30, 36, 47, 48, 54 and 59. The comfort station has showers and flush toilets, but no laundry.

Local Attractions

Pukaswka's charm is in its remoteness, so daytripping to surrounding communities is not an attraction of the park.

Fast Facts

Campground: 67 campsites in one campground (29 sites with hydro hookups); some sites are wheelchair accessible; 3 walk-in sites in campground; 32 backcountry sites. Comfort stations with showers and flush toilets (wheelchair accessible). Camping season mid-May to early September; backcountry camping year-round. No reservations taken.

Supplies: Some supplies available at Heron Bay (5 km). Better shopping is available in Marathon (13 km).

Facilities:
Trailer sanitation station
Boat launch
Beach
Interpretive centre
Hiking trails (three trails totalling about 4 km; overnight camping on 60-km trail)

Winter Use: The park is closed in winter.

Contact Information: Heron Bay ON, P0T 1R0 tel 807-229-0801

ONTARIO

Moose River

QUEBEC

631

LAKE
ABITIBI

21

17

20

TIMMINS

15

11

101

16

LAKE
SUPERIOR

129

17

144

19

14

13

12

SAULT
STE.
MARIE

18

NORTH BAY

11

17

SUDBURY

LAKE
NIPISSING

GEORGIAN
BAY

69

NORTHEASTERN ONTARIO

LEGEND

11 Samuel de Champlain Provincial Park
12 Marten River Provincial Park
13 Halfway Lake Provincial Park
14 Finlayson Point Provincial Park
15 Kettle Lakes Provincial Park
16 Ivanhoe Lake Provincial Park
17 Wakami Lake Provincial Park
18 Pancake Bay Provincial Park
19 Lake Superior Provincial Park
20 Obatanga Provincial Park
21 White Lake Provincial Park
22 Nagagamisis Provincial Park

Northeastern Ontario

Samuel de Champlain Provincial Park

Location: 50 km east of North Bay, between the
    Mattawa River and Highway 17.
Natural Environment: 2   Activities: 3   Campground: 2

If Samuel de Champlain Provincial Park is not on your itinerary for a trip to Northeastern Ontario, then it certainly should be. The park has a spectacular setting amid stately pines along 5 km of the pristine Mattawa River. Energetic and creative naturalists present visitors with an inviting array of activities that highlight the historic and natural significance of this protected waterway. From dog-sledding to guided tours aboard huge voyageur freighter canoes, every visitor can find something to do in this 2,550-ha park. Samuel de Champlain is also home to the Canadian Ecology Centre, an innovative lodging and programming facility for groups seeking education and recreation in an outdoors paradise.

Natural Environment and History

The Mattawa River is magnificently scenic—broad and deep, with picturesque sheer cliffs and rapids—as it runs from Lake Nipissing to the Ottawa River along a geologic faultline that dates back 600 million years. Equally beautiful is the forest of splendidly straight white pines that tower over jack pine, hemlock and yellow birch. Although much of the southern portion of the park was thoroughly logged during the 1880s, small areas of virgin timber remain in the remoter, northern reaches of the park.

Botanists explore the park to see an unusual hybrid of wild rye and bottlebrush grass that grows nowhere else but in this park. Wild rose, cardinal flower and other beauties lend their colour and fragrance to the park. Wildlife abounds in Samuel de Champlain. Over 200 species are named on the park's bird checklist, among them loons, wood ducks and many warblers. Larger animals include moose, bear, deer and wolves.

Although the photogenic wilds are reason enough to visit Samuel de Champlain Provincial Park, the paramount role played by the mighty Mattawa in Canadian history is another. The spirit of Champlain, voyageurs and other early explorers is a palpable presence nourished by the canoeists who paddle the length of the river each year. The Mattawa was a veritable highway for the fur trade, with convoys of up to 50 huge freighter canoes journeying together the 2,000 km between Montreal and Fort William on Lake Superior. It could well be that these tough adventurers trod the same paths that are used today by campers.

Special Activities

Waterway exploration is the best way to see the park, since there are 64 km of canoe routes along the Mattawa and connecting waterbodies. The Mattawa itself is tame enough for most levels of paddlers, except during times of high water. Boating and swimming are enjoyed on Moore Lake, and there are boat launches and three beaches in the campground. (Motorboats are limited to 10 horsepower or less.) Pike, pickerel, bass, herring and catfish are present for fishermen to catch on Moore Lake, and Long Lake has a brook trout hatchery. No motorboats are allowed on Long Lake since it is the park's source of drinking water. Canoe rentals are available from area outfitters.

Hikers can also have a day in the sun on six wonderful trails. Special features include the marsh observation platform on the one-kilometre Wabashkiki Trail. The Red Pine Trail (2.5 km) has excellent views of the Mattawa River, and also passes by Long Lake and tiny Coco Lake. The Red Pine is the shortest loop of the Etienne Trail's three loops, the longest being 9 km in length. The Kag Trail (2.5 km) has a vigorous climb up to an outstanding view of forested hills.

The staff at Samuel de Champlain are determined to keep everyone busy with what some call the best interpretive program in Ontario. The smorgasbord of daily events includes campfires, children's activities, guided hikes, instructional programs, movie and slide shows, and baseball games.

A highlight of a stay in the park is a river trip taken aboard replica voyageur canoes (Sundays through Wednesdays). Travel in an 8-metre "north" canoe and follow the route trodden by voyageurs of old. Knowledgeable guides dressed in period costume recount the stories of the fur traders and the adversities they surmounted. Given the scenery of sheer cliffs, rapids and verdant forest, cameras are de rigeur. Two different three-hour tours are available; each has spectacular scenery and no portages. A longer, six-hour paddle is also offered; it requires some stamina and fitness over six portages. The itinerary is enticing, and landmarks en route include the romantically named Porte de l'Enfer (the Gate to Hell, an aboriginal ochre mine), Talon Chutes (the bane of the voyageurs), Paresseux and Elm Point.

Another summer highlight is the Canoe Rendezvous in July. This is a busy weekend of hikes with costumed interpreters, classes in everything from wilderness first-aid and canoe repair to paddling, and a huge canoe convoy (with escort) along historic fur routes.

The park has a new voyageur heritage centre, an excellent museum with canoes, voyageur garb, and sample packs to test your mettle as a fur-trader. Maps, journal accounts, photographs and other items make the day of the voyageur come alive.

Samuel de Champlain Provincial Park is the home of the Canadian Ecology Centre, a facility comprising 34 cabins, a central dining and programming building, labs and meetings rooms. The Centre has a breathtaking array of specialty programs for social, school or business groups wanting some education with their wilderness, or vice versa. The cabins are rented out to families and individuals as well, and come with complete programming each day, such as classes in GPS (Global Positioning System), night-vision technology, hiking, canoeing, parabolic sound recording and painting pictographs. The centre is busy hosting computer eco-camps, elderhostel, digital photography education and a fabulous array of art courses with a nature slant. Children's programs are also offered. Nature study in a comfortable environment at affordable prices—an idea whose time has come.

Campgrounds

The park has 216 sites in two campgrounds. Jingwakoki's campsites are within a pine forest (shady but lacking in undergrowth for visual privacy) and Babawasse's campsites (many with hydro hookups and trailer-sized) are in a more open aspen and shrub area. Both campgrounds have beaches on Moore Lake and comfort stations. Babawasse is recommended only if you require a very large site or require hydro hookup; of the sites here, the best are numbers 13 and 14. Jingawakoki is the better campground. Beach access is terrific from sites 173, 166 and 168. Good lakeside sites are 80 to 82 (all pull-throughs), and sites 118, 120, 173 and 193 (193 is especially private). Also recommended are sites with odd numbers from 123 to 143; these are along the Amable du Fond River and the noise of the rapids may bother light sleepers.

Local Attractions

The Ottawa Valley is just waking up to its exceptional tourism potential. One of the newest attractions is the Timber Train, which takes riders on a one-day roundtrip from Mattawa through the Ottawa Valley to Temiscaming, Quebec (65 km one-way). Once in Temiscaming, you have several options, including the popular tour of a high-tech pulp and paperboard mill followed by a tour of the town centre, museum and waterfalls.

To the west of the park is North Bay, with the home of the Dionne quintuplets and *Chief Commanda II* cruises on Lake Nipissing. (See Marten River Provincial Park.)

Fast Facts

Campgrounds: 215 sites in two campgrounds (73 sites with hydro hookups); some sites wheelchair accessible. Group camping. Seasonal leasing. Comfort stations with flush toilets and showers, laundry (all accessible). Cabins available at Canadian Ecology Centre. Camping season mid-may to late September. Reservations recommended for all sites on long weekends.

Supplies: Firewood and ice sold in the park. Modest supplies at outfitters near the park. Better shopping in Mattawa (about 13 km) or North Bay (50 km).

Facilities:
Trailer sanitation station
Boat launch and dock
Canoe rentals
Beaches
Voyageur musuem
Hiking trails (four trails totalling 14.5 km)
Voyageur canoe trips daily Sunday to Wednesday

Winter Use: The park is open all winter. The Canadian Ecology Centre has programs in dog-sledding, winter camping, cross-country skiing and snowshoeing.

Contact Information: Box 147, Mattawa ON, P0H 1V0
tel 705-744-2776; Canadian Ecology Centre 705-744-1715

Marten River Provincial Park

Location: 56 km north of North Bay on Highway 11.
Natural Environment: 2   Activities: 1   Campground: 2

The best place to appreciate Ontario's magnificent old-growth white pine forests is Marten River Provincial Park, where you can pitch your tent at the foot of a 100-metre-tall, 150-year-old pine with a trunk too big around to hug. A short drive away is the Temagami White Bear old-growth forest, once the subject of controversy, now protected for future generations. While tourists and naturalists are the visitors of today, a century ago logging was the region's primary industry, and the park has a replica logging camp of over 10 buildings. Good hiking and birdwatching, along with swimming, fishing and canoe-tripping opportunities continue to make Marten River a popular park for short or long stays.

Natural Environment and History

Marten River is not a large park, but its 400 ha can feel like a much larger expanse because the park is relatively undeveloped and undisturbed. In addition, through an extensive network of canoe routes, Marten River provides access to thousands of hectares of forest and waterways.

The landscape of the park is typical of Northeastern Ontario, with rounded granite hills topped with the familiar silhouette of white pine. The forest is the province's prettiest, a mix of old pine and equally venerable yellow birch; the ghostly colour of the birch contrasts with the surrounding bright green foliage. Low-lying land supports cattail marshes and black spruce bogs. This habitat diversity and the relative quiet of the park means that the birdwatching can be excellent. The trees are alive with flitting warblers, woodpeckers, nuthatches and chickadees. Grouse are also common in the forest, and hawks soar high in the sky. Canoeists are likely to see many species of ducks, loons, grebes and heron.

Special Activities

Marten River is part of the Temagami canoe-route system that provides access to many lakes and rivers with relatively few portages or difficult sections of paddling. Wilderness outfitters located near the park and in Temagami provide maps, canoes and other supplies. From the park you can enjoy a wonderful three-day paddle that travels Marten River, Marten Lake and Wickstead Lake. Experienced paddlers can portage from Wickstead Lake to Bruce Lake and McPhee Lake. This route crosses the Nipissing Game Preserve, a great place to see wildlife of many kinds, especially moose.

Those who prefer to travel by foot take advantage of the park's 5-km hiking trail. The trail follows the edge of a black spruce bog, has an overlook over the Marten River, and takes hikers under the shade of a 300-year-old white pine that escaped the attention of early 20th-century loggers.

Throughout the park, huge stumps of pine bear silent witness to the years of logging. It was fewer than 100 years ago that these forests resounded with the shouts of loggers, the thunder of toppling forest giants, and the whirr of saws. Marten River Provincial Park celebrates that era through a replica logging camp that represents the woodsman's life of the boom years in logging—from the late 1800s to the early 1900s. Nine buildings include bunkhouses, a blacksmith shop, cookhouse, and manager's office. Equipment commonly employed in the bush is displayed along a path.

Marten River has a modest interpretive program of nature walks, evening slide shows, movie nights and tours of the logging camp. A highlight of the summer is Lumberjack's Days in mid-July, when camps, contests and demonstrations take place.

Campground

Marten River Provincial Park has 192 campsites (62 with hydro) in two distinct campground areas, one for sites 1 to 114 and a second campground for sites 115 to 192. A central comfort station serves both campgrounds. It's a joy to camp in a park where the roads are largely paved and thus dust levels are lower.

The campground with sites 1 to 114 is on the river and has a boat launch. This campground has many beautiful sites, especially numbers 33, 41, 43, 77, 81, 82 and 83. The electrical sites in this campground could vie for the title of nicest in the province, particularly numbers 2, 6 and 7.

The campground that contains sites numbered 115 to 192 is also on the river, though the sites directly across the river from Highway 11 could experience significant truck noise. The sites here are otherwise beautiful and spacious. This campground has a beach, boat launch and easy access to the hiking trail. The best sites here are 135, 148 and 151 (all on the water) and numbers 162 and 163 inland.

Local Attractions

Marten River is close to the Nipissing Crown Game Preserve, lands that are excellent for spotting a moose or doing some birdwatching. The preserve roadways are also good for mountain biking.

Marten River Provinical Park is a half-hour drive from beautiful Lake Temagami and its lovely inlets and islets that beckon to boaters and canoeists. (See Finlayson Point Provincial Park.)

North Bay is three-quarters of an hour south of Marten River, and its beaches make for a terrific picnic spot. The *Chief Commanda II* provides several different narrated cruises on Lake Nipissing; they are from 1.5 to 5 hours in length, and some excursions are dance cruises. The Dionne quintuplets' original log home was moved from nearby Corbeil to North Bay, and it is open to the public with exhibits on the famous Quints.

Fast Facts

Campgrounds: 190 campsites in two campgrounds (62 sites with hydro hookups); some wheelchair-accessible campsites. Group camping. Seasonal leasing. Comfort station with showers, laundry and flush toilets (wheelchair accessible). Camping season mid-May to late September. Reservations recommended for hydro sites all season.

Supplies: Firewood sold in the park. Convenience items and basic grocery shopping just outside the park entrance. Shopping is available at Temagami (40 km).

Facilities:
Trailer sanitation station
Several boat launches, docking
Beach (parking, barbecues)
Hiking (one trail totalling 4.8 km)

Winter Use: The park is closed in winter.

Contact Information: Marten River ON, P0H 1T0 tel 705-892-2200

Halfway Lake Provincial Park

Location: 90 km northwest of Sudbury on Highway 144.

Natural Environment: 2   Activities: 3   Campground: 3

"Summertime and the living is easy." The familiar lyrics could have been written for Halfway Lake Provincial Park, where campers of all descriptions find it easy to enjoy Canadian Shield scenery north of Sudbury. A beautiful broad beach, extensive hiking trails and superior programming are among the park's diverse delights. Halfway Lake's campground is designed to maximize campsite privacy while supplying a multitude of camper conveniences such as a store, canoe rentals, an outdoor theatre and a nature centre. Add to this a location conveniently close to Sudbury's many attractions, and you have a park suitable for long-stay holidays or for use as a base for regional daytrips.

Natural Environment and History

Halfway Lake is in the forested, lake-speckled scenery adored by Ontarians, although the park's immediate setting is more steep and hilly than much of Northeastern Ontario. Of the park's 20 lakes, Halfway Lake is the largest, but smaller jewels await discovery by hikers and canoeists.

As with many northern parks, the forest grows more lushly in the valleys where soils from glacial deposits are more fertile than the barren rocks of higher elevations. The park has a few large, majestic white pines that survived the logger's axe, though much of the park is covered in jack pine forest, an indicator that forest fire was present in earlier decades. The park's many bogs support the usual community of fascinating plants, such as carnivorous sundew and pitcher plant, sphagnum moss, Solomon's seal, cranberry and black spruce. Moose are commonly seen in the park, and other inhabitants include wolf, fox and beaver. While the bird life is not rich or diverse, campers enjoy spotting osprey, loons, pine warbler, broad-winged hawk and barn swallow.

Although the region's earliest inhabitant were aboriginals who used the beach at Halfway Lake as a summer fishing and hunting camp, it is the loggers of the early 20th century that gave the land its name. The lake, it is speculated, was halfway between the main logging area and the railway where the cut logs were loaded for transport to mills.

50

Special Activities

Travel by paddle and by foot are the best means to see the park's unspoiled interior.

Four hiking trails permit access to several remote lakes. Visitors who walk all four trails in one season are given an award badge. Park staff provide an excellent map of the park and the trails.

Moose Ridge Trail (2 km) introduces hikers to the watery world of the moose; Echo Pond (5 km) leads hikers to a lovely, quiet pond. Osprey Heights (4.3 km) is an invigorating ascent to an observation deck overlooking Antrim Lake. Loons and ducks are mere specks on the lake's surface and birds of prey soar at eye level. The park's longest trail is 15-km Hawk Ridge; many campers take two days to complete this trip, which traverses four interior lakes and provides excellent opportunities for wildlife viewing.

The park rents canoes, and whether you rent or bring your own, you'll find Halfway Lake's interconnecting waterways make for an excellent outing. The portages in the park are well marked and well maintained, and there are kilometres of leisurely paddling.

Boating is permitted on Halfway, Antrim and Bailey Lakes; the boat launch is near the campground. Fishing is popular in the park, and pickerel and pike are the species most commonly caught.

Halfway Lake has a kilometre-long beach with warm water that stays shallow a fair distance from shore. It's perfect for sandcastle building, waterplay and sunbathing, and the huge playground, volleyball court and tether-ball court are popular. Picnic and barbecue facilities, a sophisticated amphitheatre, and a campfire area round out the beachfront offerings.

The visitor centre has informative displays and hands-on activities related to local flora and fauna. Children's contests and games are run from the centre, and staff lend dip nets to budding field naturalists. Park staff honestly earn their reputation for friendliness and high energy. The very active interpretive program has events scheduled twice daily for much of the summer, and is sometimes even busier on weekends. Typical events include guided hikes, fishing derbies, campfires, and workshops on canoeing, orienteering and forest-fire fighting.

Campground

These may be the best-designed campgrounds in Ontario. The sites are spacious, private and well spread out. Wild Rose Campground has

85 hydro sites mainly for trailers; all have electricity. Campers in sites closest to Highway 144 may find traffic noise a nuisance; a good plan is to reserve the sites farther from the highway, which are in general the higher-numbered sites. Sites 67 and 69 are especially good.

Hawksnest Campground has sites numbered 86 to 215; many of these also have electricity. Sites 88 to 91 overlook Raven Lake. Sites farthest from the beach are most quiet, and of these, sites 127, 129, 131, 136 and 137 are very good. Other recommended sites include 174, 180 and 185. These recommendations being made, it is useful to note that Halfway Lake does not have an undesirable campsite.

This is a park that takes its creature comforts seriously. Each of the three comfort stations has showers, flush toilets and laundry. The camp store rents canoes and sells groceries, camping needs and ice cream.

Local Attractions

Halfway Lake is the choice location for a holiday that combines authentic outdoors adventure with the attractions of a city. Sudbury is less than an hour's drive from Halfway Lake, and offers a first-rate facility in Science North, which is really three attractions in one: the science centre, the IMAX theatre, and an area devoted to virtual adventure rides. Science North is a fabulous experience for the whole family, a science centre with displays and hands-on experimentation in everything from veterinary science to earthquakes yet compact enough to see it all in one day. Don't miss the various demonstrations on kitchen chemistry, lasers and northern animals that take place throughout the day; young science students bring a refreshing enthusiasm to their topics. Best of all, many of the displays relate directly to the northern environment.

The IMAX theatre shows whatever movies are currently making the rounds and the virtual adventure rides provide the thrill of a roller coaster with high-tech effects. Science North has a snack bar and a full-service restaurant that overlooks pretty Ramsey Lake. Boat cruises on Ramsey leave several times daily from the dock near Science North.

Sudbury is famous as a hard rock mining town. At the Big Nickel Mine, guides conduct 45-minute tours that take place 20 m below ground. Mining technology, explosives and underground safety are discussed. Above ground, displays and hands-on activities focus on mine operation and prospecting. Every tourist takes a snapshot of the 9-m-tall "Big Nickel."

Fast Facts

Campgrounds: 215 sites in two campgrounds (120 sites with hydro hookups); some sites wheelchair accessible. Group camping; 50 backcountry sites. Seasonal leasing. Comfort stations with showers, laundry, flush toilets (wheelchair accessible). Camping season mid-May to late September. Reservations recommended July and August.

Supplies: Firewood and ice sold in the park. The park store sells groceries and there is an ice-cream stand. Supplies also available in Onaping (about 30 km).

Facilities:

Trailer sanitation station

Trailer/boat storage

Boat launch but no docking

Canoe, paddleboat, waterbike and bike rentals

Sports equipment for loan

Volleyball court

Beach

Playground

Nature centre

Hiking trails (four trails totalling 26 km)

Bike path (5 km)

Winter Use: The park is closed in winter.

Contact Information: 199 Larch Street, Suite 404, Sudbury ON, P3E 5P9 tel 705-965-2702

Finlayson Point Provincial Park

Location: 96 km north of North Bay in the village of Temagami.

Natural Environment: 2   **Activities:** 2   **Campground:** 1

Finlayson Point is a boater's dream come true: a campground with easy dockage and deep water on one of Northern Ontario's largest and prettiest lakes. Although this is a postage-stamp park—only 94 ha—it provides access to a huge expanse of wild country. Lake Temagami is "big water" in this region of countless tiny lakes, and the lake is wonderful for exploration by boat or canoe because of its irregular shoreline and countless islands. When boating loses its appeal, nearby hiking trails can take you through the region's famous old-growth forest or to a forest fire tower.

Natural Environment and History

Finlayson Point may be a small park but it is on Lake Temagami, one of Ontario's great scenic treasures. Temagami is an Objiway word for "deep waters by the shore," an apt description of a shoreline that has many rocky, sheer cliffs. The lake covers over 20,000 ha of water and has over 1,300 islands, from tiny islets that provide root-hold for a few blueberry bushes and a pine tree to large islands with several cottages.

Loggers cleared the forests here from the late 19th century through to the Second World War, though the less-accessible stretches of Lake Temagami still protect stands of white pine that are 200 years old; they grace the horizon with their characteristic wind-bent silhouette. Red pine, yellow and white birch, spruce, strawberries and blueberries also grow here. Open meadows in the forest are beautiful with the abundant wildflowers that bloom in white, yellow and orange all summer long.

The forests support plentiful wildlife populations, and bear and moose are common in the region, as are many smaller mammals. In Finlayson Point Provincial Park proper, only the smaller mammals are seen. Birds observed in and around the park include the loon, osprey, warblers, mergansers and heron.

The forested hills and waters that support wildlife have supported human populations for centuries. Some portages in the region have been dated, from archaeological evidence, to over 3,000 years in age; other estimates put human habitation to over 6,000 years. More recently, lumberman settled here, as did miners seeking gold and silver. With the coming of the railway, cottaging became more common, as did wilderness outfitting and guiding. One of the region's best-known residents was Grey Owl, the legendary Englishman (born Archie Belaney) who became one of the 20th century's greatest conservation writers.

Special Activities

Unlike many parks, where travel by foot is the norm, Finlayson Point is boat country, and the fully serviced boat harbour, launches and docks are the primary reasons many campers return to the park annually. It takes many days to explore even a small portion of Lake Temagami because of its long shoreline and many "arms," or large bays and inlets. The fishing here can be rewarding, and though lake trout are the usual prize, whitefish, pike, pickerel and bass also inhabit the lake.

The park has limited recreation facilities, but the two small beaches have floating platforms and are very busy. The park also has a playground. Finlayson Point has no interpretive programming.

Lake Temagami and canoe tripping are almost synonymous. The lake itself provides days of exploration possibilities, and canoeists based in the park find themselves well located to explore waters northwest of Lake Temagami, such as Lady Evelyn-Smoothwater Wilderness Park and four other waterways that provide routes of varying difficulty and length. Local outfitters are well able to supply all equipment and supplies, especially the maps and descriptions of paddling conditions in the four major waterway parks in the greater Temagami region. Air transport companies fly fishermen and canoe trippers into remote lakes for daytrips or longer stays.

During the winter, the entire region is a winter playground, and has extensive networks of ski and snowmobile trails. Some of the trails in the park are groomed, though there are no facilities for winter camping.

Campground

The campground is located on a tiny peninsula just outside the town of Temagami. Given its size and water-bound situation, the 114-site campground has a remarkable diversity of campsites. Some are small and open, others are large and shaded; many have direct access to shoreline, and none are far from the boat docks and beaches. Thirty-three sites have hydro hookups. Some of the best sites are 11, 12, 32, 107B and 114. All of these are on the water, and those closest to docking areas might experience more boat noise. Inland sites are more spacious, private and shaded; examples of these sites include numbers 42 and 66 to 68.

Local Attractions

Temagami is increasingly well known as the home of the White Bear Forest, a protected area of red and white pine forest with trees 150 to 350 years in age. The trees are not only huge, but have a stately beauty owing to their size and remarkably straight trunks. Hiking trails criss-cross the forest, and excellent canoeing opportunities exist on adjacent lakes. The main part of the forest is most easily accessed by boat, and outfitters in Temagami ferry hikers to prearranged drop-off and pick-up points.

Caribou Mountain is the region's highest point of land, and the view from the mountain encompasses the town and park, as well as distant vistas of forest and lakes. On a clear day it is possible to see as far as Maple Mountain, 56 km to the northwest. The trails on the mountain vary in length from 400 m to 6.5 km in length. Although driving almost to the summit is possible, walking and biking are even more rewarding means of ascent. Signs at the summit describe efforts being made to re-establish peregrine falcons on the mountain heights. The fire tower is newly renovated to permit public access to an observation platform at the top.

Temagami's fish hatchery is a volunteer project that restocks lakes with pickerel that are hatched and reared to fingerling stage at the facility on Lakeshore Drive. Depending on the timing of their visit, tourists may see fish hatching from eggs or young fish being fed. The hatchery hosts a fish derby held annually in midsummer.

Fast Facts

Campgrounds: 114 sites in two campgrounds (33 sites with hydro hookups); some sites wheelchair accessible. Comfort station with showers, laundry, flush toilets (wheelchair accessible). Camping season late May to late September. Reservations recommended for hydro sites all season and for all sites in July and first two weeks of August.

Supplies: Firewood and ice are sold in the park. Supplies are easily obtained in Temagami, just outside the park.

Facilities:
Trailer sanitation station
Seasonal storage of trailers/boats
Boat launch and docking
Complete marina services
Canoe rentals
Boat rentals very close to park
Beach
Playground
Hiking trail (one trail, 5 km from park to top of Caribou Mountain)

Winter Use: The park is closed in the winter, but visitors make use of over 100 km of ski and snowmobile trails that run through the park.

Contact Information: Box 38, Temagami ON, P0H 2H0
tel 705-569-3205

Kettle Lakes Provincial Park

Location: 40 km east of Timmins off Highway 101.
Natural Environment: 1   Activities: 2   Campground: 1

Ten thousand years ago, glaciers began their retreat from Ontario's land-scape, and left behind in their wake enormous ice blocks buried beneath a layer of soil and rock. In the Timmins region of Northeastern Ontario, these prehistoric ice blocks slowly melted to form circular depressions that are now deep, brilliantly turquoise lakes surrounded by birch and aspen forest. Twenty-two of these lakes lie within Kettle Lakes Provincial Park, and furnish excellent swimming, good novice-level canoeing and a pretty backdrop for campsites. Visitors enjoy a good interpretive pro-gram, hiking trails and summertime relaxation in a family-oriented environment. Kettle Lakes is well situated as a base camp for travellers wanting to take in the famous gold mine tours in Timmins.

Natural Environment and History

From beginning to end, the landscape of Kettle Lakes is a product of glaciation. Unlike other parts of the north that were stripped bare dur-ing the ice ages, Kettle Lakes Provincial Park received sand and gravel from the glaciers, as well as huge boulders (called erratics) seemingly strewn across the land. The landscape here tells a story of glaciation, and of human history as well. Loggers deforested much of these 1,200 hectares in the early 1900s, and reforestation restored the original spruce and fir of the boreal forest as well as aspen, birch and pine. Jack pine and aspen mark the location of a forest fire that raced through here in the 1920s.

Kettle Lakes Provincial Park is known for its abundance of wildflow-ers and lesser plants, which means you can visit the park in May, July and September and see completely different species in bloom. Forest-dwelling species include lichens and wintergreen, while the lighter shade under aspen and birch trees allows the growth of honeysuckle, devil's paintbrush, clintonia and sarasparilla. Spruce and tamarack bogs support leatherleaf, Labrador tea, sphagnum moss and pitcher plant.

The park has several wetlands, including a floating bog, within its boundaries, and two non-kettle lakes, Hughes and Mud Lakes. Unlike the steep-sided and rocky or sandy kettles, these natural lakes have plenty of aquatic vegetation along their shores that provides habitat for fish and forage for moose. Other mammals in the park include bear, fox, beaver and hare. Birds are also attracted by the lakes, and commonly sighted species include heron, woodpeckers, gulls, ducks and loons.

Special Activities

No other northern park can boast six different beaches on six different lakes—you can visit a different one on each day of your visit: Slab Lake (a great beach with playground), Paxton Lake, Green Lake, Point Lake, Irrigation Lake and Island Lake. Three of the beaches are large and attract the majority of campers, while the other three are small and more private in atmosphere.

Hughes and Mud Lakes are the only waterbodies where you can use a motorboat. (Hughes Lake has a boat launch.) Fishing on these lakes may garner a pike, trout or bass; several lakes are stocked with trout. The absence of motorboats, and the sheltered calm of the kettle lakes means that these are excellent places for beginners to master their J-strokes. Longer distance canoeing is impossible since none of the kettle lakes have incoming or outgoing rivers—each is a watery "island."

The park has five walking and hiking trails, several with information signs along the way. The walking trail, also popular with cyclists, follows the main park roadway for its 3.5-km length and is a safe alternative to walking on the road. There are four interpretive trails: Tamarack (2 km), Oh-Say-Yah-Wah-Kay (3 km), Kettle Lake (4 km) and Wintergreen (3 km). Particularly interesting is the Tamarack Trail, the easiest of the four to walk. Visitors are introduced to life in a northern bog and the gradual succession from bog to black spruce forest.

The visitor centre is the place to find out about organized activities such as guided hikes, children's crafts, sports nights, games and campfire night. The centre also has displays on the park environment.

The park remains active during the winter, and cross-country skiers, snowshoers and ice fishermen use the trails and lakes.

Campground

Two campgrounds, Island Lake and the Pines, have a total of 137 camp-sites (83 with hydro hookups). The two campgrounds share a comfort station and are equally close to the amphitheatre. Island Lake is the main park campground, the location of all electrical sites, and a popular choice for those who want to be close to a large beach. The campsites at Island Lake are in young forest so there is not much visual privacy here, and the sites are closely spaced together. In general, the higher-numbered electri-cal sites have the greatest undergrowth near them. Site 57 may be the most private of the non-electrical sites.

A more laid-back atmosphere prevails at the Pines campground, which has no electrical or large trailer sites. A modest 21 sites overlook Bullfrog Lake. Although these are also open sites, the small number and spacing mean that these are desirable for those seeking a quieter camping experience. In particular, sites 12 and 17 to 19 are recommended.

The park has a snack bar and store for basic necessities. Most shopping needs can be met in Timmins (40 km) or in Iroquois Falls (20 km).

Local Attractions

Kettle Lakes Provincial Park is perfectly located to take advantage of the interesting tourist attractions of Timmins. The best of these is the Timmins Gold Mine Tour. Experienced miners lead groups of tourists (outfitted in work overalls, helmets, miner's lights and boots) underground about 150 feet where demonstrations and discussions portray life underground during past decades. Above ground there is a cafeteria, an art gallery and gift shop.

Fast Facts

Campgrounds: 137 campsites in two campgrounds (83 sites with hydro hookups); some sites wheelchair accessible. Group camping. Comfort stations with showers and flush toilets and laundry (only toilets wheelchair accessible). Seasonal leasing. Camping season mid-May to mid-October. Reservations recommended for all sites from mid-June to September, especially on long weekends.

Supplies: Firewood and ice sold in the park. Shopping available in Iroquois Falls (20 km) and Timmins (40 km).

Facilities:
Trailer sanitation station
Boat/trailer storage
Boat launch but no docking
Beaches
Playground
Horseshoe pits
Playing fields
Visitor centre
Hiking trails (five trails totalling 15.5 km)

Winter Use: The park is open mid-December to mid-March and has 30 km of ski trails, snowmobiling, snowshoeing and ice fishing.

Contact Information: Box 3090, South Porcupine ON, P0N 1H0
tel 705-363-3511

Ivanhoe Lake Provincial Park

Location: About 100 km west of Timmins, off Highway 101.
Natural Environment: 2   Activities: 2   Campground: 1

In the early 1900s, the mills in the Foleyet region of Northern Ontario produced railway ties. Loggers from these mills, while working on the dam at the outflow of Ivanhoe Lake, accidentally re-arranged the course of the Ivanhoe River and drained the lake. What may sound like an environmental disaster created several extraordinary features now protected by Ivanhoe Lake Provincial Park. Two of these features, a lakeshore panne and a quaking bog, are rarely found treats for naturalists. The third feature, a 3-kilometre strand of pure sand, is Northern Ontario's very best beach and is the delight of travellers and campers alike. Ivanhoe Lake Provincial Park is popular for family holidays, fishing trips and canoe outings.

Natural Environment and History

The park's 1,500 hectares encompass not only Ivanhoe Lake but many delightfully tranquil smaller lakes as well. The scenery is typical of Ontario's rocky north, with several notable exceptions, all of them relics of the glacial past. For natural scientists first and foremost is the "panne," an unusual plant community that grows in conditions of low nutrients and high lime concentrations. The panne in Ivanhoe Lake Provincial Park is located close to the beach area, and was originally lake-bottom until exposed by lowered water-levels.

The park's "quaking bog" is a mat of small plants and shrubs that actually floats on the surface of a pond; the name refers to the way the mat shakes when touched. Bog plants include the pitcher plant and sundew, which survive in this acidic, nutrient-deficient environment by consuming insects. This particular bog is growing in one of the park's several kettle lakes, created when blocks of glacial ice melted to create deep, round depressions that filled with water. Ivanhoe Lake's lovely beach is yet a third creation of the glaciers, which dumped the sand here when they retreated. It wasn't until the loggers re-arranged the drainage patterns in the region that these features were exposed.

Campers enjoy viewing the many species of wildlife in the park, such as moose, beaver and bear. Other boreal species include several types of owls and hawks.

Special Activities

Most activity in the park takes place in or around the water. Ivanhoe Lake beach is a real find, easily the most spectacular strand in the entire north. Three kilometres of pure sand, hard and rippled very far from the shore, with shallow, warm swimming for all ages. The beach area is backed by sand dunes (another rarity in the north). The main day-use area has a playground, picnic tables, comfort stations and parking.

At one end of the beach is a boat launch, and boating and sailing are popular on large Ivanhoe Lake. Canoeing is better done on Saw Lake, where motorboats are prohibited. This long, island-studded lake is very pretty, with plenty of good picnic spots. Saw Lake's sheltered setting means that canoeing conditions are excellent for novices. Peaceful Teck Lake is also worthy of exploration by foot or by water. The lakes in this park are productive of fish: pike, pickerel and whitefish are caught in Ivanhoe Lake, and Saw and Teck Lakes are stocked with brook trout.

Ivanhoe Lake Provincial Park has three short hiking trails. The Saw Lake Trail (2.8 km) traverses the gravel ridges left by glaciers and follows the shoreline of beautiful Saw Lake. Quaking Bog Trail (0.8 km) has interpretive signs that explain the formation of bogs and identify some of the plants and animals found here. The Teck Lake Trail (1 km) leads through boreal forest of fir and spruce near Teck Lake.

Ivanhoe Lake park staff are justifiably proud of their diverse programming, which is administered with a large dose of good humour. Children's programs include talks on nature (from predators to butterflies), crafts, games and wild snacks. Evening programs often feature guest speakers and slide shows or movies. Canoe hikes, guided hikes, campfires, star-gazing nights and bike hikes round out the program. Each August the staff host an Edible Wilds Food Feast when campers can sample foods such as wild game and fish, wild teas, cattail casserole and other goodies.

Campgrounds

A total of 120 campsites (64 electrical) are provided in several different campgrounds. The campgrounds share two comfort stations, each with showers and flush toilets. In general, campsites close to the beach are convenient, but they have less shelter and are less private than sites inland. The campsites in Red Pine are a short walk from one of the best parts of the beach, but are very open sites, best suited for trailers. All 24 sites here have electrical hookups, except for numbers 25 to 29, which are exposed to the traffic on the main roadway, but have fewer neighbours.

The Le Rivage Campground has densely spaced sites in a sand-dune setting. More suited for trailers, all these sites have electricity. The best of these sites are numbers 30 to 32. The White Birch Hill Campground is away from the water. These sites (numbers 70 to 92) are very secluded and private, though they can get buggy. Sites 90 to 92 are farther from amenities but close to good canoeing on Saw Lake. The La Baie Campground (numbers 93 to 120) are also closely spaced, but some of the sites are the best in the park, especially numbers 93, 95, 99 and 101.

Local Attractions

The city of Timmins is located about one hour away from Ivanhoe Lake Provincial Park. Its attractions include an underground gold mine tour. (See Kettle Lakes Provincial Park.)

Fast Facts

Campgrounds: 134 campsites in four campgrounds (63 sites with hydro hookups); some sites are wheelchair accessible. Group camping. Seasonal leasing. Comfort stations with flush toilets, showers and laundry (only toilets wheelchair accessible). Camping season mid-May to mid-September. Reservations recommended for long weekends and for electrical or beachfront sites.

Supplies: Firewood and ice sold in the park. Basic groceries and convenience items are sold at local lodges. Better shopping in Foleyet (14 km).

Facilities:
Trailer sanitation station
Trailers/boats storage
Boat launch but no docking
Beach
Playground
Hiking trails (three trails totalling 4.6 km)

Winter Use: The park is closed in winter.

Contact Information: 190 Cherry Street, Chapleau ON, P0M 1K0
tel 705-899-2644

Wakami Lake Provincial Park

Location: 145 km northeast of Sault Ste. Marie on Highway 667.
Natural Environment: 3   Activities: 1   Campground: 3

Wakami Lake Provincial Park is breathtakingly beautiful, a picture-postcard scene of sparkling azure waters embraced by rolling hills and verdant forest. The vista stretches south from the campground as far as the eye can see—over 8,700 ha of unspoiled, unsettled wilderness. This haven for wildlife and breathing space for campers has plenty of possibilities for outdoor fun, from hiking to birdwatching, swimming to fishing.

Natural Environment and History

Wakami Lake is a transition zone between north and south in more than one way. The park is on the continental divide that separates waters that flow south to the Great Lakes from the waters that drain north to Hudson Bay. North and south also meet in the park's landscape. This park lies in the transition zone between northern boreal forest and southern mixed forest. Although spruce and fir is predominant, trees more typical of temperate environments grow here as well: red pine, yellow birch and maple. Low-lying areas include true northern bogs (floating mats of spaghnum moss), shallow marshes alive with ducks and heron, and beaver meadows thick with tall sedges and wildflowers.

At one time the region was dominated by forests of huge white pine; however, logging companies removed most of the virgin timber during the first half of the 20th century. Campers gratefully note that sapling white pines are making a comeback in the park.

This mixed forest provides habitat for an equally diverse wildlife population. Given the remoteness of the park and the quietness of the campground, wildlife of many species are readily observed close at hand. Moose and bear are common here, as are mink, beaver, porcupine and marten. Birds of interest include osprey and bald eagle; both of these species are commonly seen in the park and are attracted to Wakami Lake by the healthy fish population.

Special Activities

Fishing is indeed very good at Wakami, and you can try your hand for pike, pickerel and whitefish on Wakami Lake and pike and speckled trout on Imakaw Lake. The park has a boat launch, a fish-cleaning hut and a fish smoker.

There are four short hiking trails near the campground and one long-distance trail. They are the Transitional Trail (2.5 km), the Beaver Meadow Discovery Trail (2.4 km), and the Hidden Bog Trail (4 km). Each of these brings hikers into a different habitat type, from boreal forest to northern bog.

One of the most strenuous long-distance trails in Ontario is Wakami Lake's Height of Land Trail. It travels 75 km in a loop around the lake and takes four to five days to complete. Besides the great scenery, the trail allows access to many points of interest such as an abandoned trapper's cabin (and perhaps a Hudson Bay outpost), aboriginal gravesites, and deserted logging equipment and camps. Hikers must make arrangements for their Height of Land expedition ahead of time, because boat transport across the northern arm of the lake is necessary. Wakami Lake provides 20 interior campsites for use by backcountry explorers.

Canoeists love Wakami's quiet bays. For longer paddles, try the Wakami Lake Canoe Route, a 56-km route that takes three or four days to complete. Although there are portages and several lakes to canoe along the way, the route is considered a good one for novice paddlers. Another (unnamed) canoe route travels 100 km south of the park to Ivanhoe Lake Provincial Park. The park has a large, shallow beach area that is never too busy since it serves so few campers.

Wakami Lake and region boast a proud logging heritage. A tremendously informative Historic Logging Exhibit paints a vivid portrait of life in backwoods logging camps. Historic photographs, maps, diagrams and plenty of equipment from the days of horsepower and brawn are found in displays situated along a one-kilometre trail. Best of them all is a "diary" detailing daily life in the camps, complete with colourful descriptions of homemade lice remedies, lack of sanitation, and long days of difficult work. This is one of the best information displays in the provincial park system.

Wakami's modest interpretive program has the usual elements, such as guided hikes, evening activities and campfires. The visitor centre features changing displays on topics such as logging and trapping. The highlight of the summer takes place annually in late July. During Woodsmen's Days, there are contests for the entire family, from log sawing to seed spitting. Most of the activity takes place in the beach area, and though this is an event that draws mainly from the locale, the atmosphere is fun and friendly for everyone. During the corn roast and a wonderful evening spirit hike, costumed staff take on roles as characters from logging days.

Campground

This campground at Wakami Lake has only 65 sites (none with electric) that are spread over four areas. Sites 1 to 14 are suitable for large trailers, but are completely lacking in privacy and are closely spaced. Sites 17 to 20 in Pine Grove have good views of the lake and adequate privacy. While all of sites 21 to 54 in Brown's Bay are good, sites 55 to 59 are exceptional. These sites have their own water access, and the water is shallow enough that you can wade out and sunbathe on several huge boulders. Because these sites are close to the shallows of Brown's Bay, the nearby woods and shores teem with black duck, heron, gulls and loons.

Local Attractions

Wakami Lake is quite isolated from any major community. When visiting the park, it is probably best to plan on spending all your time on the trails or on the lake.

Fast Facts

Campgrounds: 65 site in four campgrounds; 20 backcountry sites. No comfort stations. Seasonal leasing. Camping season mid-May to late September. Reservations usually not necessary, except for the weekend of Woodsmen's Days in July and on long weekends.

Supplies: Firewood sold in park. Basic supplies at Sultan (10 km). Better shopping at Chapleau (62 km).

Facilities:
Trailer sanitation station
Boat launch and docking
Fish smoker
Beach
Playground
Visitor centre
Hiking (four trails totalling 9 km; overnight hiking on a 76-km trail)

Winter Use: The park is closed in winter.

Contact Information: 190 Cherry Street, Chapleau ON, P0M 1K0
tel 705-233-2853

Pancake Bay Provincial Park

Location: 76 km north of Sault Ste. Marie
between Highway 17 and Lake Superior.
Natural Environment: 2   **Activities:** 1   **Campground:** 1

Ask any resident of North Central Ontario or Michigan the location of their favourite campground, and the largest number will likely answer Pancake Bay Provincial Park. The park's main draw is a 3-km beach of the finest white sand in Northern Ontario—a rarity on Lake Superior's shoreline of wave-battered granite. In the shallow water protected by two headlands, Superior's icy coldness warms to a barely acceptable temperature by midsummer. The park is a preferred haunt of boaters because of its calmer waters and nearby launching facilities. The park also offers hiking trails, including one to a high lookout over the shore, where you may see the spot where the ill-fated *Edmund Fitzgerald* sunk.

Natural Environment and History

The beach is the most noteworthy feature of this 4,990-ha park. The beach's length and very fine white sand make Pancake Bay a beloved holiday spot for generations of families and a welcome rest stop for those driving on the Trans-Canada. Two headlands protect the beach from the erosive power of Lake Superior's swells. Inland, the park is part of the Algoma landscape of mixed forest. White and red pine, yellow birch, cedar and maple are the commonest trees in the canopy, while undergrowth includes hazelnut and a wide variety of berries. The most abundant wildlife are many species of warblers and woodpeckers, as well as such small mammals as beavers, muskrats and chipmunks.

The name Pancake Bay dates to the days of the fur-trading voyageurs. This sheltered bay would be the paddlers' last stop before reaching the end of their long journey at Sault Ste. Marie. Low on supplies, they would have only flour remaining for their last meal, and thus pancakes was the choice for dinner.

Special Activities

While many visitors spend entire holidays swimming, sunbathing and building sandcastles, the park is a venue for other activities. Boating is a common pastime here, though boats must be carried to the shore or driven to a boat launch 11 km north of the park to the mouth of the

Batchawana River. Spring and fall are productive times for fishermen to try landing a rainbow or lake trout.

The park has two hiking trails. A 3.6-km route brings hikers through several habitat types, including a cedar swamp and wetland that is particularly good for unusual vegetation. Another trail highlight is a gargantuan "erratic," a boulder deposited here more than 100,000 years ago by a retreating ice sheet. Throughout the camping season, berry picking (and eating) is also a favourite endeavour.

A longer, 12-km hike takes you to the lovely Pancake River and Pancake Falls, as well as through marshes and wonderful forests. This trail, popular with campers and daytrippers, uses stairs to access two observation platforms high above Pancake Bay and Whitefish Point. Whitefish Point is the location where the lyrically immortalized *Edmund Fitzgerald* sunk in 1975. Park publications provide details on the tragedy.

The highlight of Pancake Bay's interpretive program is the annual Pancake Days in August, which offers three days of pancake breakfasts, a fish fry, contests and games that include sandcastle building and baseball. Later in August, campers are taken for free rides in 36-foot-long freighter canoes similar to those used by voyageurs. Fly-fishing lessons are given on both of these special weekends.

Many outfitters in the Pancake Bay vicinity supply the equipment and lessons for guided or self-guided adventures. Ask park staff for local companies specializing in sea kayaking and canoeing.

Campground

Pancake Bay has 329 campsites (109 with electricity), all of them in close proximity to the beach. The campground has several comfort stations and playgrounds. The campsites are rather cramped compared to those in other provincial parks, and more open as well, but this does not diminish the popularity of the park with its loyal users. The electrical sites closest to the beach include sites 347 to 372 and sites 151 to 160 (the latter are also close to a playground, a comfort station and the amphitheatre). The non-electrical sites closest to the beach include sites 229 to 241 and 457 to 478. Sites 1 to 90 are farthest from the main beach areas, but have good access to a hiking trail, a playground and a comfort station.

Local Attractions

Pancake Bay is a handy base for exploring the beautiful Algoma country made famous by the Group of Seven. One of the best ways to see a lot of breathtaking wilderness in a day is the 114-mile train trip through the Agawa Canyon. The train travels through the steep-sided canyon (a geologic fault formed 1.2 billion years ago), climbing heights, descending valleys and passing over the curving 1,550-foot-long Montreal River trestle. A two-hour stopover allows for hikes to the canyon top (300 stairs) or to several spectacular waterfalls. Two trips leave daily during the summer, and one leaves daily on winter weekends. Autumn excursions to view the best foliage colour in eastern North America are especially popular and should be booked well in advance. Visitors who want to spend a few magical days living in the heart of Group of Seven country can reserve the Canyon View car—a fully equipped railcar accommodating up to four—permanently located on a rail siding.

Sault Ste. Marie has two historic sites of interest. The Canadian Bushplane Heritage Centre is located in an operational 1940s hangar, and celebrates the history of bushplanes and wilderness firefighting.

The Sault Canal National Historic Site has guided tours that cover the history and technology of the canal built to bypass the St. Mary's River rapids. (The historic canal is now a recreational waterway.) There is a visitor centre, a 2-km trail with self-guiding signs and a gift shop. Boat tours of the modern locks allow close-up views of legendary 1,000-foot lake freighters.

The rapids that made the canal and locks necessary provide for some of the best fishing in the world. Resident rainbow trout and whitefish, and migratory salmon, steelhead and brown trout provide plenty of action along the rapids from May through October. Also on the waterfront is the M.S. *Norgoma*, once a passenger ship, now a museum dedicated to the heyday of steamships.

Fast Facts

Campground: 329 sites in one campground (109 sites with hydro hookups). Group camping. Seasonal leasing. Comfort stations with showers, flush toilets and laundry (wheelchair accessible). Camping season early May to mid-October. Reservations usually not necessary.

Supplies: Firewood and ice sold in the park. Modest supplies at local restaurants. Best shopping is in Sault Ste. Marie (76 km).

Facilities:

Trailer sanitation station

Boat launch 11 km north of park

Trailer/boat storage

Beach

Playground

Hiking trails (two trails totalling 18.6 km)

Winter Use: The park is closed in winter.

Contact Information: Box 61, Batchawana Bay ON, P0S 1A0
   tel 705-882-2209

Lake Superior Provincial Park

Location: About 130 km north of Sault. Ste. Marie along Highway 17.
Natural Environment: 3   Activities: 2   Campground: 1

A remarkable array of backcountry experiences awaits the fortunate visitor to Lake Superior Provincial Park. View ancient pictographs painted on wave-pounded rocks; hike through steep valleys to remote waterfalls; explore ghostly fishing villages; ride the fabled Algoma Central Railway into the heart of the Agawa Canyon. The scenic splendour of the region made it a favourite subject of the Group of Seven, and the forested hills and lakeshore beckon modern-day artists and photographers. Although the park's three campgrounds are situated close to the busy Highway 17 corridor that traverses the park north to south, the solitude and majesty of the wilderness are easily accessible to all visitors.

Natural Environment and History

Lake Superior Provincial Park protects a huge area (1,556 square km) of the dramatic Algoma landscape beloved by artists. The landscape seen today—mountainous and wild as it is—is actually a tamer version of what volcanoes created eons ago. Glaciation, earthquakes and erosion rounded jagged mountains into steep-sided hills, and wide faults are now canyons and shoreline cliffs.

Lake Superior Provincial Park is wonderfully diverse because it has southern forests of sugar maple and yellow birch and northern forests dominated by white spruce and white birch. In park lowlands, black spruce and tamarack are prevalent. In open areas along Lake Superior, early summer brings a beautiful bloom of wildflowers that includes unusual subarctic species.

Moose are common throughout the park. Black bear and timber wolves also inhabit the park, although Lake Superior does not support the density of bears that other northern parks do. One hundred and twenty bird species are known to nest in the park, and many others visit the park during migration. Bald eagles are often seen along the rivers during fall, attracted by spawning salmon.

The land within the park has been home to indigenous people since at least 9,000 BC. The park is the site of at least one archaeological mystery, the Pukaskwa Pits—depressions made over 2,000 years ago along cobble beaches. Red-ochre pictographs, or rock paintings, occur at several sites within the park and are most easily seen at Agawa Rock. Trapping and fishing were important livelihoods into the 1900s, and the region has a long history of tourism and outpost guiding.

Special Activities

Lake Superior Provincial Park is a dream come true for hikers. The 55-km Coastal Trail follows the Lake Superior shore between Chalfant Cove and Sinclair Cove. Trail conditions encompass pebble beaches and rocky headlands, challenging scrambles over gigantic boulders, and steep woodland paths. Coastal Trail veterans recommend fall excursions for the spectacular foliage display and the absence of biting insects. It is advisable to plan on taking a week to traverse the entire trail, in order to make allowance for foggy and wet weather, both of which can make rocky sections treacherous. Special permits to use the trail campsites are necessary. A highlight of the trail is the abandoned fishing village of Gargantua Harbour. Although all that remains of this 19th-century fishing community are portions of the pier and the warehouse, the scene of weathered buildings set in a peaceful cove is charming indeed.

The park has ten shorter trails, and excellent trail descriptions are found in a brochure available at the park office or the visitor centre. The following trails are frequently recommended. Orphan Lake Trail (8 km) has lookouts over tiny Orphan Lake and mighty Lake Superior. The trail includes an excellent lunch stop at a pebbled beach and a return hike past the falls of the Baldhead River. Nokomis Trail (5 km) is a strenuous ascent to fabulous views of the 200-metre-tall cliffs known as Grandmother (Nokomis). Nokomis Trail is also the place to visit the mysterious Pukaskwa Pits. For a heart-pounding climb, Awausee Trail (10 km) and Peat Mountain (11 km) both ascend steeply to provide two views, the first of the Agawa River valley and the second of glistening Lake Superior. The most popular trail is that to Agawa Rock. Although only a half-kilometre in length, this can be a demanding trek in rough weather, especially for young children. The trail passes through narrow chasms and over boulders to reach a narrow ledge over dashing waves. It is at this point that you may view the red ochre pictographs.

Paddlers enjoy daytrip or multi-night adventures on the park's innumerable lakes and rivers. Although there are some easy routes (the 16-km Fenton-Treeby Route is popular), most overnight routes are challenging, with long, rugged portages around whitewater. Experts rave about the Lower Agawa Canyon (two days) and the Anjigami River (five days). Both kayakers and canoeists enjoy the numerous sheltered bays of the Lake Superior shoreline. Only experienced adventurers should travel on the open waters of Lake Superior, as unpredictable weather can create treacherous conditions without warning.

Lake Superior and the park's numerous lakes and streams provide wonderful wilderness fishing for lake, brook and rainbow trout, whitefish, and salmon, and many hikers catch lunch along the trails. Motorboats are prohibited in the park, except for on Lake Superior, and on Sand Lake, where motors of no more than 10 horsepower are permitted.

Interpretive programs operate from the Agawa Bay and Rabbit Blanket Lake Campgrounds. Campers young and old enjoy evening slide shows and films, campfires with skits and stories, young naturalists' programs and evening guided hikes. The Friends of Lake Superior Park have a store and office in the Agawa Bay campground. The store sells park merchandise, books, and tickets for the Agawa Canyon Tour Train.

No park services are provided during the winter, but deep snow (averaging 4 m a season) and cold weather attract intrepid explorers for cross-country skiing, snowshoeing and ice-fishing.

Campground

Lake Superior Provincial Park has three campgrounds with 274 sites (58 electrical). Forested Crescent Lake campground is the smallest and least developed, with only water pumps and privies. Crescent Lake is excellent for a quieter camp experience (particularly site 31) and is ideal for family canoe outings. Swimmers hardy enough to enjoy Lake Superior's brisk waters head for Agawa Bay's 3-km beach. The visitor centre here has displays on the natural environment and human history of the park. This campground has electrically serviced and trailer-sized sites, although all sites here are rather open and breezy. Rabbit Blanket Lake Campground (in the northern area of the park) also has electrical sites. Many of the sites here are hilly and thus less suitable for large trailers; optimum privacy is found at sites 40 to 44. Because Peat Mountain Trail begins here, Rabbit Blanket is a good base for exploring the park's interior.

All three campgrounds are within earshot of the Trans-Canada Highway. The campsites most sheltered from highway noise are the lakefront sites in Crescent Lake Campground and the sites in Rabbit Blanket Lake Campground situated farthest from the highway.

Local Attractions

Lake Superior Provincial Park is about an hour and a half north of Sault Ste. Marie and its interesting historic sites, such as the canal and locks. The "Soo" is also the point of departure for the legendary Algoma Central Railway, a daylong train trip through spectacular scenery made famous by the Group of Seven. (See Pancake Bay Provincial Park.)

Fast Facts

Campgrounds: 249 sites in three campgrounds (58 with hydro hookups). Group camping; 175 backcountry sites. Comfort stations with showers, toilets and laundry at two of three campgrounds (wheelchair accessible). Camping season early May to early September. Reservations recommended for all sites in July and August.

Supplies: Firewood sold in the park. Some supplies and ice available near the park. Decent grocery shopping is a long distance away, so purchase main supplies before entering park.

Facilities:
Trailer sanitation station
Trailer/boat storage during summer only
Boat launch but no docking
Canoe rentals
Beach
Visitor centre
Hiking trails (11 trails totalling over 125 km)

Winter Use: The park is closed in winter.

Contact Information: Box 267, Wawa ON, P0S 1K0, tel 705-856-2284

Obatanga Provincial Park

Location: 56 km northwest of Wawa on Highway 17.
Natural Environment: 2   Activities: 1   Campground: 2

Although for many travellers Obatanga Provincial Park is simply a convenient stopping place along the busy Trans-Canada, this park warrants a much longer stay. Obatanga is an excellent base for canoe trips into serene lakes and rivers, including the challenging White River route from the park to Lake Superior. Obatanga is also prime wildlife habitat, and the chances of seeing moose are especially good. Fishing is a popular pastime at here, and there are opportunities for hiking and swimming. An interpretive program geared to all ages and excellent campsites add up to an enjoyable holiday in Northern Ontario.

Natural Environment and History

Obatanga Provincial Park is one of the larger parks in Northern Ontario, 9,400 ha of quiet forest, sparkling lakes (32 in all) and rivers that abound with fish. The topography of the park is typical of the region, with low, rounded hills and lakes surrounded by pine and small beaches.

A devastating 1910 forest fire was a major determinant of the landscape within the campground. Since fire favours the growth of jack pine, a tree with cones that open only under intense heat, this part of the park is largely an even-aged stand of jack pine. Underneath the pine grow the moccasin flower (an orchid) and, of special interest to most visitors, berries. Although strawberries and raspberries grow in the park, it is the dependably heavy crops of blueberries that garner most of the attention. In some fortuitous summers, the harvest period of all three berries overlaps. The rest of the park was spared the 1910 fire, and a typical northern boreal forest predominates. Black spruce grows in damp or wet areas, and birch, fir and aspen grown together on drier sites.

Obatanga is well known for plentiful fish and wildlife populations. Indeed, this may be the best park in Ontario for spotting moose, which visit wetlands to munch on aquatic vegetation. It may be that the large size of Obatanga and the quiet atmosphere in the park encourage visits by moose. Other park inhabitants are bear, beaver, mink, otter, and birds such as loons (common in the campground area), ruffed grouse, duck and Canada goose.

Special Activities

Obatanga was heaven sent for canoeists. Dozens of lakes and rivers await discovery, and it is possible to canoe for days without seeing another soul. Even daytrips from the campground can bring paddlers to quiet places for a few hours spent in natural beauty and solitude. Park staff can advise on the best routes. A half-dozen lakes are easily accessed by a short drive from the main campground.

Long trips can also begin in the park. The best known is the Knife and Obatanga route that leads eventually to the famous Dog (or University) River route to Lake Superior. This route takes several days and is recommended for expert canoeists. A three-day trip that is considerably less demanding is the route from Hammer Lake to Obatanga Lake. Canoe rentals are available from local outfitters.

While a canoe is the best means of transport into interior lakes, Burnfield Lake is popular for boating as well. Although pike and pickerel are easy to catch in the lakes throughout the park, the remoter lakes are often most productive of fish.

The park has a 2.4-km hike with a longer, 4.5-km loop. The Forest Fire Trail is a loop beginning and ending at Berry Trails Campground, and encircles a lilypad-covered pond that is excellent for viewing moose and ducks. The trail brochure is a good introduction to the fascinating world of acid-tolerant boreal forest plants: Labrador tea, snowberry, sphagnum moss, clintonia, bunchberry and speckled alder, to name just a few.

The park rents bikes (to adults only) for use on the level and uncrowded park roads. Staff conduct interpretive events once every two weeks. Campfires, skits and guided hikes are the most common programs.

Campground

Two separate campground areas are on Burnfield Lake with 132 campsites in total; 20 of these have hydro hookups. A central comfort station has flush toilets, showers and a laundry. The Windy Pines campground is aptly named, for the westerly wind whistles across the lake and through the campground; this helps keep these sites almost mosquito-free. This is the place to camp if you want good access to the park's long (but narrow) beach, the excellent playground and the campfire area. The electrical sites are in Windy Pines, and are very typical of those in other parks. The best campsites are away from the main swimming area, sites such as 7, 8, 11, and 12 to 15. Although sites number 13 to 23 have perfect shorelines for sunset-watching, they can receive noise from the

Trans-Canada across the lake. Quieter conditions are available at the other sites named.

The Berry Trails Campground is smaller and thus quieter in nature. It has good access to the hiking trail, a smaller beach and the boat launch. Good lakeside sites in Berry Trails are numbers 119, 127 and 128.

Local Attractions

The closest community of any size is Wawa. Outfitters in town provide fly-in trips to remote wilderness and canoe tours of the scenic Magpie River. Closer to town is High Falls, a lovely picnic spot. Just east of Wawa is a day-use facility at Potholes Provincial Park. A walking trail with interpretive signs leads visitors past pretty tumbling streams to the "potholes," round depressions carved out of the bedrock by swirling glacial meltwaters.

Fast Facts

Campgrounds: 132 sites in two campgrounds (20 sites with hydro hookups); some sites wheelchair accessible. Seasonal leasing. Comfort station with showers, flush toilets and laundry (wheelchair accessible). Camping season mid-June to early September. Reservations not taken.

Supplies: Firewood and ice sold in the park. Basic needs can be met at local lodges. Better shopping is in Wawa, 56 km away.

Facilities:
Trailer sanitation station
Trailer/boat storage
Boat launch but no docking
Canoe and bike rental (bikes for adults only)
Beaches
Playground
Hiking trails (one trail with loops of 2.4 and 4.5 km)

Winter Use: The park is closed in winter.

Contact Information: Box 340, White River ON, P0M 3G0
tel 807-822-2592

White Lake Provincial Park

Location: 35 km east of Marathon on Highway 17.
Natural Environment: 2   **Activities:** 2   **Campground:** 3

Hiking, boating, canoeing, fishing, swimming—outdoors opportunities abound in the 1,700 ha of White Lake Provincial Park. Boaters and anglers appreciate docking, boat launches and the opportunity to fish on huge White Lake, reputed to be a hotspot for angling. Canoeists appreciate the fact that the southern end of the lake is protected from high winds, and that the park provides access to several outstanding canoe routes. Swimmers head for the expansive sands of White Lake's uncrowded beach, where you can wade out for dozens of metres. The widespread popularity of White Lake is due in part to the full program of activities and events led by enthusiastic, friendly staff and in part to the well-planned and spacious campground.

Natural Environment and History

It is with great pleasure and anticipation that visitors drive along the long entranceway to the campground at White Lake. The roadway winds through beautiful large trees, part of a lush mixed forest that is a contrast to the boreal forest present in much of the rest of the region. Glaciation and location are the two main reasons for White Lake's distinctly different landscape. Although the ice ages were brutal to the rest of the north, the region surrounding White Lake is underlain by a thick layer of sand and pebbles that the ice removed from the James Bay Lowlands and deposited here. Not only does this deposit means that there is better soil to support luxuriant forest growth, but the limestone content of the glacial debris protects park waterways somewhat from the worst effects of acid rain.

The second reason for White Lake's lovely forests is that the park is sheltered from chilly Lake Superior by distance and by its situation in a sandy basin. Thus, White Lake is home to more fragile and delicate plantlife than found elsewhere in the region. Although the pine and aspen forest looks typical, underneath the trees grow 12 species of orchid, including the brilliant moccasin flower.

Aboriginal peoples such as the Cree and Ojibwa appreciated the thriving game and fish populations in the area. The beaver population that attracted the attention of 19th-century fur traders still thrives today, to the delight of hikers and canoeists. Moose, bear, mink and other mammals live in the park, as do many species of birds.

Special Activities

White Lake Provincial Park is a special favourite of boaters and fishermen. The park has several boat launches and a boat basin with docking near the campground. Boat rentals are located just outside the park. White Lake is a huge body of water, with a large northern portion connected to a small southern portion via a narrows that has some gravel shoals. The northern portion is particularly inclined to be choppy and windy while the southern portion is sheltered and more dependably calm. Other lakes in the park with good fishing include Clearwater and Deer Lake; Clearwater has been stocked with speckled trout. Live bait is not permitted in Clearwater Lake.

Several excellent canoe routes are accessible from the park. The White River canoe route (rated one of the top 10 routes in Ontario) follows White River for 72 km from the park all the way to Pukaskwa National Park on Lake Superior. The scenery en route is dramatically beautiful, with rock-walled canyons, rapids and a large waterfall. Other routes include the Kwinkwaga River route, the Depew River route and the Bremner River route. The easiest route of these is the Depew River route, which is 50 km of novice-level canoeing through typical boreal forest scenery.

The park has two hiking trails as well as a fitness trail with exercise stations. Popular Deer Lake Trail (1.5 or 2.5 km, depending on route taken) leads through jack pine forest to a pond formed by a beaver dam. The trail brochure discusses plants and animals seen en route such as reindeer moss, beaver, mink and moose. Birdwatchers visit the marsh to see common goldeneye and ring-necked ducks, marsh wren and warblers. Tiny Bog Trail is a 4.5-km hike through a northern bog where carnivorous pitcher plant and sundew share space with spaghnum moss and Labrador tea. Clearwater Trail Lake (2 km) takes walkers through a black spruce forest where trees wear garlands of the lichen called Old Man's Beard. The trail is a good place to study wildflowers, pick berries, and see beaver and moose. Clearwater Lake is a favourite subject of photographers because of its clarity and luminous green colour.

The campgrounds also have a volleyball court and horseshoe pitch, and park staff can provide sports equipment. Swimmers and waders adore the large beach and the possibility of wading far out into the lake.

Park staff run a busy schedule of events all summer long. Evening presentations at the amphitheatre, children's crafts and games, guest speakers and guided hikes are the typical components of the program. Each July the park hosts a Fishing Expo, a weekend of parades, campfires, contests and lots of fishing. Log Drive Days occurs annually in August, and involves logging and forestry contests and a spirit hike.

Campground

The campground at White Lake is well away from the Trans-Canada, and is thus protected from highway noise. The campgrounds are located at the south end of the park and overlook the narrows that link the southern and northern portions of White Lake. Three campgrounds have a total of 187 campsites and 60 of these have electricity. The electrical sites are under a pine canopy, and thus tend to be a little open, but are still well spaced apart. The non-electrical sites, however, are excellent in terms of spacing and privacy. Good sites away from the water include numbers 169 and 181 to 186, and good water's-edge sites include 80 to 82 and 84 to 90. (Number 86 may be the prettiest campsite in the province, though noise from the community across the lake can be an occasional drawback.)

Local Attractions

White Lake is 35 km from White River, where the Domtar sawmill provides public tours several times daily. Visitors watch the process of creating construction lumber from forest to finished product.

Fast Facts

Campgrounds: 187 campsites in three campgrounds (60 sites with hydro hookups); some sites wheelchair accessible. Group camping. Seasonal leasing. Comfort stations with showers, laundry, flush toilets (wheelchair accessible). Camping season mid-May to late September. Reservations recommended for electrical sites all season long.

Supplies: Firewood sold in park. Some supplies can be purchased at local resorts, but the best shopping is in White River (35 km).

Facilities:
Trailer sanitation station
Trailer/boat storage
Boat launches and docks
Canoe rentals
Sports facilities
Beaches
Playground
Hiking trails (three trails totalling 8 km, including a fitness trail with stations)

Winter Use: The park is closed in winter.
Contact Information: Box 340, White River ON, P0M 3G0
    tel 807-822-2447

Nagagamisis Provincial Park

Location: 30 km north of Hornpayne on Highway 631;
    42 km south of Highway 11.
Natural Environment: 2   Activities: 1   Campground: 2

If there is one park that should be on the holiday plans of fishermen, it is Nagagamisis. The park encompasses the remarkably clear waters of huge Nagagamisis Lake and several smaller waterbodies, each one productive of a good catch. Add to excellent fishing a long beach, sheltered waters for leisurely canoeing, and a very quiet campground, and it's easy to see why many campers return to the park yearly for their holiday. The park's location is well off the beaten track, so that it is easy to drink in the profound quiet of the forest and observe the northern lights without interruption.

To fully enjoy the park, water transport of some kind is necessary, and boat and canoe rentals are available near the park entrance.

Natural Environment and History

As with much of the province, various ice ages formed a lot of the topography of Nagagamisis. During the last ice age, a giant glacier stood at the northwestern edge of Nagagamisis Lake and deposited irregularly shaped gravel hills called kames. The more rugged hills of the southern portion of the park mark the spot where the glacier also deposited huge amounts of till.

Unlike in the rest of the north, at Nagagamisis the lusher forest grows on the well-drained upper slopes, while the poorly drained lowlands permit limited growth. The higher elevations have mature forest of fir, aspen, and white birch that provide shade and shelter for the growth of bunchberry and other shrubs. The lowland forest is characterized by alder, larch, and floating mats of sphagnum moss and Labrador tea. The most lasting impression for many visitors is that of the never-ending hectares of black spruce forest—the tree's narrow and stunted silhouette almost symbolic of the far north.

This park is rewarding for birdwatching. Many residents of Southern Ontario travel to the park to spot northern species such as pileated and black-backed woodpecker, grey jay and merlin. Spring and fall are especially recommended for the binocular set because of the park's location on two major migratory routes. Animals common in the boreal forest are often seen in the park, such as hare, beaver and fox. Moose are often seen at dusk, close to the marshy places they frequent for foraging. Viewing animals is not the only kind of nature-watching going on in the park: Nagagamisis is one of the most northerly of Ontario's parks and it is common for campers to stand and marvel at the shifting hues of the northern lights.

Nomadic aboriginals used the park for hunting, and later fur-traders harvested beaver here. A trapper's cabin and some native gravesites are within the park and are accessible by canoe or boat. These sites are protected by law.

Special Activities

Fishing is the primary activity in the park. Pickerel, pike, perch, whitefish and white sucker are commonly caught, both from boats and from the shoreline near the campground. Other lakes in the park have brook trout, splake and rainbow trout. The park provides a boat launch, dock, fish-cleaning house and a fish smoker for the convenience of campers. Boat rentals are available from nearby lodges. The use of live bait is prohibited throughout the park.

Canoeists, too, revel in the endless kilometres of quiet waterways. Motorboats are prohibited on Park Lake, so this is a good, sheltered lake for novice paddlers. The lakes in the park are remarkably clear and sometimes tempt scuba divers to explore their depths.

The park has two hiking trails. The one-kilometre Time Trail is best trod with the informative brochure in hand; it explains the different stages of forest succession seen along the route. A longer, 4-km trail is also available; it leads along the shore of both Nagamisis and Park Lakes. Campers often make use of the park roads, which are traffic-free, as additional routes for exercise, birdwatching and plant-finding. (Park staff lend out plant identification guides.)

The beach at Nagagamisis, a residual from the last ice age, is a long strand of sand mixed with pebbles. There is a buoyed area for swimming, although the drop-off to deep water is close to shore.

Campground

The campground is on a narrow peninsula between two lakes, well situated for viewing the colourful sunsets and northern lights for which the park is renowned. Many of the 86 unserviced sites are close to the water's edge, and many are reserved seasonally. The campsites are of average size and are medium to densely spaced. As is usual, the better sites are close to the water's edge. These are sites 36 to 48 (even numbers only) and sites numbers 130 to 156 (even numbers only). Inland sites that are more private and spaced farther apart include sites 20 to 24.

Camper amenities include a comfort station with showers, flush toilets and a laundry. Church services held in the campground chapel each Sunday.

Local Attractions

The charms of Nagagamisis—deep solitude, northern plants and animals, spectacular beauty—are enjoyed more deeply because of the park's remote location. That remoteness, however, means that it's a long drive to any attractions. Hornepayne (33 km) is the closest community; it offers a swimming pool and shopping. Hearst (100 km) has a recreation centre with a pool, an art galley, tennis courts and a golf course. White River (136 km) offers sawmill tours provided by Domtar. (See White Lake Provincial Park.)

Fast Facts

Campground: 86 sites in one campground; some sites wheelchair accessible. Seasonal leasing. Comfort station with showers, laundry, flush toilets (all accessible). Camping season mid-May to late September. Reservations not taken.

Supplies: Firewood and ice sold in the park. Basic supplies available at local outfitters (15 km). Best shopping in Hornepayne (33 km).

Facilities:
Trailer sanitation station
Boat launch and docking
Boat rentals available near the park
Trailer/boat storage
Fish smoker
Beach
Hiking trails (one trail totalling 1 km)

Winter Use: The park is closed in winter.

Contact Information: Box 670, Hearst ON, P0L 1N0 tel 807-868-2254

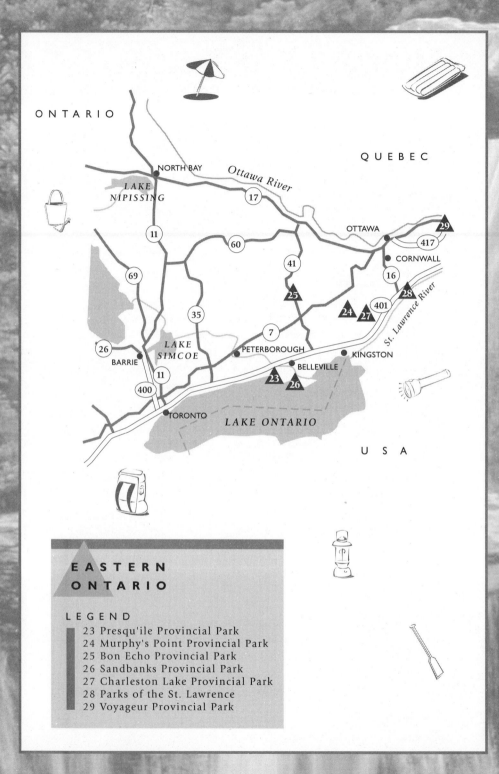

ONTARIO

QUEBEC

NORTH BAY

Ottawa River

LAKE
NIPISSING

17

OTTAWA

29

11

60

417

CORNWALL

41

16

69

25

28

24 27

35

401

St. Lawrence River

7

LAKE
SIMCOE

PETERBOROUGH

26

BARRIE

KINGSTON

11

BELLEVILLE

400

23 26

TORONTO

LAKE ONTARIO

U S A

EASTERN ONTARIO

LEGEND

23 Presqu'ile Provincial Park
24 Murphy's Point Provincial Park
25 Bon Echo Provincial Park
26 Sandbanks Provincial Park
27 Charleston Lake Provincial Park
28 Parks of the St. Lawrence
29 Voyageur Provincial Park

Eastern Ontario

Presqu'ile Provincial Park

Location: 7 km south of Brighton on Lake Ontario.
Natural Environment: 1   **Activities:** 3   **Campground:** 1

Presqu'ile Provincial Park is an invaluable remnant of natural Lake Ontario shoreline, a narrow triangle of land that juts bravely into the waves. Presqu'ile protects several shoreline and wetland habitats and the wildlife that lives here year-round or uses the peninsula during migration. Birdwatching is a favourite pastime at Presqui'ile, evidenced by the bird-sighting bulletin board at the park entrance. Monarch butterflies also attract wildlife lovers each September as the butterflies congregate here during their annual trek to Mexico. The park's sophisticated interpretive centre highlights the glamorous celebrities—mostly rum-runners and pirates—who plied these waters decades ago. Presqu'ile's sandy beach is a popular spot for swimming, boating, boardsailing, walking and cycling.

Natural Environment and History

While many Great Lakes parks are known for their long, sandy beaches, Presqu'ile Provincial Park is more remarkable for the diversity of its shoreline environments. The park encompasses sand and pebble beaches, extensive marshlands, wooded swamp, sand dunes and limestone bluffs. Each of these environments is habitat to a unique assemblage of plants and animals.

Most important, Presqu'ile is a known for its outstanding bird habitat. Over 125 species of birds nest in the park, and another 200 or so species stop here to rest and feed in preparation for migration. This peninsula is a critically important resting and feeding place for thousands of migrating plovers, whimbrel and sandpipers, and nesting habitat for several species of shorebirds such as the spotted sandpiper. Sections of the sand beach are roped off to prevent disturbance of breeding shorebirds. High Bluff and Gull Islands, just off the park's tip, are home to over 200,000 birds, the largest colony of gulls and terns on the

Great Lakes; these islands, too, are off limits from mid-March to mid-September. Even outside the breeding season, the islands and the beach are popular for birdwatchers looking for the elusive purple sandpiper.

The expansive marsh along the eastern shore of the park is home to numerous species of amphibians; salamanders and snakes inhabit the nearby damp forest. The marshlands, like the beaches, are important staging grounds for large rafts of ducks in spring and fall. During peak migration, birdwatchers line up to observe over 10,000 ducks of 25 species at one time, among them common goldeneye, oldsquaw, canvasback and bufflehead.

The forest at Presqu'ile is lively with warblers, catbird, thrushes and other songbirds all season long. Panne, or wet meadows, support a delightful wildflower bloom, along with sparrows and other open-land species.

Special Activities

Presqu'ile's large sand beach has plenty of space for sunbathers, swimmers, volleyball players and walkers. The park store, which sells groceries, ice cream, fast food and souvenirs, is not far from the beach. A bike path runs almost the entire length of the park from the northern entrance to close to the Chatterton Point, where cyclists may join up with Lighthouse Lane to access the nature centre and the Lighthouse Interpretive Centre.

The winds off the peninsula are excellent for sailing and windsurfing, and a boat launch is provided. Boats and windsurfers are restricted from the designated swimming area.

Presqu'ile's interpretive program has so many first-rate events that it draws large numbers of day visitors as well as campers. First and foremost are the events for birdwatchers—special weekends year-round that feature birding workshops, bird banding, art shows, children's activities, tea rooms and evening presentations. A history weekend in August presents games and contests, a sailing regatta and a drama. Each fall there is a Monarch butterfly tagging weekend and a deer research workshop.

Special activities are held daily during the summer and on weekends during spring and fall. These may include guided hikes, movies and slide shows, dramatic presentations, campfires and children's crafts and games. Many activities take place in the nature centre run by the Friends of Presqu'ile or at the Lighthouse Interpretive Centre. Both of these facilities have excellent displays. The nature centre has many live animals and exhibits on local ecology. The interpretive centre has multimedia displays on park history, especially the exciting years of Great Lakes rum-running.

Presqui'ile has approximately 10 km of cross-country ski trails, though snow cover may not permit much skiing in some winters.

Campground

Four campgrounds have a total of 394 campsites (24 electrical). There are comfort stations with showers, flush toilets and laundries at several places in the park. As with many lakeside parks, the campsites here are quite open and lacking in privacy. The exception at Presqu'ile is Craig's Campground, where large sites are located in a verdant forest of ferns, ash, oak and maple. Craig's also has the advantage of being a radio-free zone. The best sites here are numbers 175 and 177.

All electrical sites are in the rather crowded Pines Camground, and the best of these are sites 121 to 124. Although densely designed, some sites in Presqu'ile have nice water views; these are numbers 213, 215, 216, 333 and 335 and 371. Elmvale Campground has two nice sites farther from the water: 283 and 285. Trailers requiring a pull-through will head for High Bluff, although these sites lack privacy and have high density. All sites near the water have good access to the bike path.

Local Attractions

Presqu'ile is surrounded by daytripping country—numerous villages with great shopping, farm markets and fall fairs, theatre and museums. Brighton is in the heart of apple-growing country, and its September Apple Fest offers a street market, modest midway, and tours of orchards. The entire Northumberland County area is a treasure trove for antique hunters. In particular, Port Hope and charmingly historic Grafton have dozens of top-notch shops. Port Hope is also the location of the Capital Theatre, designed in 1930 as the first movie theatre in Canada. Tours are available. Cobourg's Victoria Hall is the epitome of mid-19th-century grandeur. This courthouse and municipal building is a must-see for its lavish trompe-d'oeuil paintings and sunken courtroom modelled after London's Old Bailey.

Fast Facts

Campgrounds: 94 campsites in eight campgrounds (24 sites with hydro-hookups); some wheelchair-accessible sites. Group campsites. Comfort stations with flush toilets and showers (wheelchair accessible). Camping season early April to late October. Reservations recommended for all sites in July and August and on all long weekends.

Supplies: Firewood and ice sold in park. Park store sells some groceries as well as fast food and ice cream. Best shopping is in Brighton (5 km).

Facilities:

 Trailer sanitation station

 Trailers/boat storage

 Boat launch just outside park, dockage at local marinas

 Beach

 Interpretive centre

 Nature centre

 Bike path (5 km)

 Hiking trails (one trail totalling one kilometre)

 Church services

Winter Use: The park is open year-round and has about 10 km of cross-country ski trails and winter camping.

Contact Information: RR 4, Brighton ON, K0K 1H0 tel 613-475-4324

Murphy's Point Provincial Park

Location: 19 km south of Perth off Road 21.

Natural Environment: 1 **Activities:** 2 **Campground:** 2

Situated along a large peninsula on Big Rideau Lake, Murphy's Point Provincial Park is an exceptional home base for excursions along the Rideau Waterway by car or by boat. With 1,200 hectares of forest and several lakes, Murphy's Point has plenty of room for swimming, fishing, canoeing and hiking. The park's spacious and well-planned campgrounds are among the nicest in the province. While many parks include local history as part of their education programs, Murphy's Point takes visitors into the heart of the matter through fascinating tours of the abandoned Queen Mine that produced mica during the early years of the 20th century.

Natural Environment and History

Murphy's Point has a hilly profile, and those hills are covered with two distinct forest types: in some areas northern trees such as spruce and fir are most common, while the farthest reaches of the peninsula are covered in maple, beech and oak forest. Wildlife populations in the park reflect the diversity of the plant community. Deer, racoon, porcupine and hawks are commonly seen, and owl and coyote also inhabit the park. The park's wetlands teem with life—beaver, muskrat, turtles, great blue heron and several species of duck.

Murphy's Point was settled early in Ontario's development and it is an excellent place to bear witness to the first farming and industry in the region. Early settlers, like the Murphy family of Ireland, created backwoods homesteads on level lands farther from the lakeshore. McParlan House (a restored log home) and the remains of a sawmill both date to the early 1800s. The Lally homestead of log cabin, outbuildings and snake-rail fence sits amid wild meadows—a scene as poignant and photogenic as you'll find anywhere.

Murphy's Point is best known for its industrial past. Mica, apatite and feldspar were were mined in the region. The park protects the Silver Queen mine, and park staff conduct tours down into the mine during the summer.

Special Activities

Murphy's Point Provincial Park is a great place to enjoy watersports. Boating is a primary activity on Big Rideau Lake, and boat launches and dockage are available. Many boaters head out into the Rideau Waterway, using the locks of the canal to access kilometres of blue lakes. Most boaters take their fishing tackle with them to try for a legendary Rideau fighting bass, or for a pike or lake trout.

Canoeing and sailing are most pleasant on Loon Lake and Hogg Bay, where powerboats are not permitted and the water is screened from high winds. Several campsites in the park are accessible only by water, sheltered in quiet coves for use by boaters or canoeists. Paddlers trace a route that begins on Loon Lake, travels around the Murphy's Point peninsula, and ends at Hogg Bay.

The park has 15 km of hiking trails, with levels of difficulty and length for every hiker. The best part of hiking at Murphy's Point is that every trail meanders past a small beach, so that any hike can include a picnic and swim. Particularly secluded swimming spots can be discovered on the 5.5-km Point Trail and the 2.5-km Sylvan Trail. The McParlan Trail leads across the pretty rapids of Black Creek to the McParlan homestead, which is open to visitors and has displays on local history. A 6.5-km section of the famous Rideau Trail (300 km from Kingston to Ottawa) runs through the park; the trail can be accessed from the end of the McParlan Trail.

An active activities program has events scheduled daily during summer and weekend events during spring and fall. Commonly activities are hikes, children's activities, campfires with storytelling, movies and guest speakers. Special flower and birding days take place during the spring; days of music, food and crafts are scheduled for autumn.

The highlight of a stay in this park is a guided tour into the Silver Queen mine. Visitors don yellow helmets and descend into the cool mine to see sparkling mica and other minerals, and the ferns and other shade-dwellers that can eke out a living in the limited light. Above ground, the tour includes the interior of a recreated miner's barracks.

Fun in the sun doesn't stop with summertime. Cross-country ski enthusiasts trek along 30 km of groomed trails, and snowshoers can explore the silent beauty of 1,200 ha of winter wilderness. A ski chalet and warm-up hut are provided. January is the time for the annual loppet.

Campground

Two campgrounds have a total of 187 campsites (25 with hydro). The campgrounds are spacious and well planned, with comfort stations with flush toilets, showers and laundries. The Hogg Bay Campground is closest to the main beach. This campground has hydro sites and many pull-through sites for trailers. Sites 40 to 46 are especially recommended, as are sites 61 and 65. The Fallows Campground is more hilly and forested in nature, and has many excellent sites. In particular the following are spacious and private: 103, 108, 110, 29, 136, 137, 142, 147, 149, 150, 156, 175, 184, 189, 193 and 194. Sites 113 and 114 are well suited for two groups camping together.

Loon Lake Lodge, available during the off-season, has accommodation for up to 30 people, and park staff run interpretive programs for interested groups staying in the lodge.

Local Attractions

Murphy's Point is in the centre of a region renowned for antique shops, art galleries and charming limestone villages. Lovely Perth, known to historians as the best collection of limestone buildings west of Montreal, is just 22 km from the park, and is well worth a daytrip. Matheson House Museum has displays on local history, including the pistols used in Canada's last duel, a contest fought in Perth (1833). North of Perth stretches Lanark County, land of textile mills (and legitimate factory outlet shops), cheese factories and small town dairies.

Thirty-two kilometres northeast of the park is another canal town, Smiths Falls. Hershey Canada hosts self-guided tours of their chocolate plant; a store is on the premises. Smiths Falls also is home to the outstanding Rideau Canal Museum. This handsome stone building has five floors of displays, hands-on exhibits and historic documents that bring the history of the canal to life.

Fast Facts

Campgrounds: 168 sites in two campgrounds (26 sites with hydro hookups); some wheelchair-accessible sites. Group camping; 12 backcountry sites; 30-person lodge available to groups off-season. Comfort stations with showers, laundry and flush toilets (wheelchair accessible). Camping season mid-May to mid-October. Reservations recommended for all sites all summer long.

Supplies: Firewood and ice sold in the park. Supplies available in Perth (22 km).

Facilities:

Trailer sanitation station

Trailer/boat storage

Boat launch and docking

Canoe rentals

Beaches

Playground

Hiking trails (six trails totalling 23 km)

Winter Use: The park is open all winter and has extensive cross-country trails. Ski chalet, warm-up hut, January loppet.

Contact Information: RR 5, Perth ON, K7H 3C7 tel 613-267-5060

Bon Echo Provincial Park

Location: 30 km north of Highway 7 on Highway 41, between Belleville and Algonquin Park.

Natural Environment: 3   Activities: 3   Campground: 2

Bon Echo—the very words conjure up so many images of wilderness that the park has almost mythic status in Ontario. One of the province's most-photographed natural wonders is Mazinaw Rock, a 100-m-tall, 1.5-km-long face of dark rock that plummets into deep, blue Mazinaw Lake. Aboriginal red-ochre pictographs painted on the cliffs are one of North America's largest groupings of these ancient word-images. Bon Echo also includes over 6,000 ha of mixed forest and pristine lakes, the passion of backcountry hikers, bikers and canoe trippers seeking natural solitude. Mazinaw Lake itself is the pleasure of boaters, fishermen and swimmers.

Natural Environment and History

In ways both obvious and subtle, it was geologic events that gave Bon Echo its unusual features. Mazinaw Rock was created from molten rock about 20 km beneath the Earth's surface about one billion years ago. Hundreds of millions of years later a massive re-arrangement of the Earth created a fault, or split, in the rock along a north-south line. The cliff side of the fault rose high above its matching twin, and the intervening precipitous drop became Mazinaw Lake, which although only 1.5 km in width is about 150 m deep, making it the deepest lake in Eastern Ontario. The lake's mysterious depths are not its only remarkable feature. The fault separating looming Mazinaw Rock from the park is very narrow, barely allowing passage of a pleasure cruiser. Thus, it is easy to paddle across to the rock to explore its heights.

Bon Echo is in a region that includes both northern and southern elements in an intriguing mix of plants and animals. Northern inhabitants include white and red pine, spruce and bearberry, along with raven, wolves and moose. Southerners present in the park include red oak, beech, hop hornbeam, five-lined skink and turkey vulture.

The magnificence of Mazinaw Rock came to early notice, and the rock face was a canvas for over 200 red images painted by Algonkian-speaking peoples. The images can best be seen by canoe. (Please do not touch the paintings.) Later, farmers made futile attempts to work the thin soils and rock outcrops of the Canadian Shield. Most farms failed and people moved on; remnants of their work and their communities remain to be discovered by hikers. More recently a luxury hotel, the Bon Echo Inn, occupied land across the lake from the rock. Although the hotel was destroyed by fire, its celebrity owner and guests contributed colour to local history, and are given special place in evening dramatic presentations by park staff.

Special Activities

Bon Echo is a watery place indeed, and it is to the park's several lakes that most visitors head. Everyone makes their first outing a walk to the point of land opposite Mazinaw Rock, where they crane their necks to study its looming presence. The Mugwump Ferry carries visitors across the narrow channel to a walking path and stairway that lead up the cliff face to the top (2 km). The view from the top takes in tiny figures on the sandy

peninsula below as well as the expanse of Bon Echo's lush forests. According to the Clifftop Trail brochure, those forests comprise 9 million trees of 35 species. The informative brochure also discusses other features seen en route, such as prairie warblers, red oak barrens, blueberries, and birds of prey.

The park has many other excellent hikes, all with good self-guiding brochures. The Shield Trail is a 4.8-km loop that includes the remnants of the Addington Road, one of Upper Canada's notorious colonization roads built to encourage farming and settlement in the harsh conditions of the Canadian Shield. The High Pines Trail is a 1.6-km trek through white pine forest and a hemlock wintering-yard used by deer. Beavers, kingfishers and other wetlands denizens are easily viewed along the one-kilometre Bon Echo Creek Trail, a favourite with young families. Long-distance hikers head out along the 17-km Abes and Essens Lakes Trail, which has several hike-in camping sites. This trail can also be enjoyed as a day hike, since it has shorter loops of 4 km and 9 km.

Bon Echo has a large beach with fine sand and good swimming. Motorboating and fishing are popular on the lake, and the park has two excellent boat launches and a dock. Pickerel, pike, bass and lake trout are the prizes on Mazinaw Lake. Boats and other equipment are readily available from local outfitters near the park. Guided tours of Mazinaw Lake on the *Wanderer Too* leave the park dock daily.

Motorboats are prohibited on the park's interior lakes, which remain unspoiled canoe-tripping territory. Indeed, Bon Echo canoe trips have turned many a child into a dedicated naturalist. Joeperry and Pearson Lakes have a total of 25 canoe-in sites. A very popular, six-hour paddle is the Kishebus Canoe Route (21 km including a 1.5-km portage) a circular route that traverses many of the park's most famous features. Canoe rentals are available in the park and from local outfitters.

Campers need never run out of things to do. Activities are planned for each day and most evenings during the peak summer camping season. Children's programs are designated for particular age groups, meeting for pond studies, salamander searches, puppet shows, crafts, games and stories. Everyone is invited to movies, slide shows, talks by visiting naturalists and dramatic presentations. Bon Echo's campers have hymn sings and non-denominational church services each Sunday.

The Greystones gift shop sells souvenirs and books related to Bon Echo and nature in general. The visitor centre has changing displays on the geology and ecology of the park, as well as on local history.

Bon Echo is an active place during the winter as well, and skiers and snowshoers explore a brilliant white wilderness of perfect peace.

Campground

Bon Echo's popularity is due in part to its excellent campground facilities. Mazinaw Lake Campground has 430 campsites (132 with hydro hookups), several comfort stations, and close proximity to the beach, the boat launch, most hiking trails, the visitor centre and other amenities. The campground has three areas. Sawmill Bay has the most private campsites in a hilly and wooded setting. Particularly good are sites 23, 25, 27, 29, and 60 to 68, 135 and 137. The following have water views: 115, 116, 118, 120, 121 and 122. Wonderful sites (with terrific rocky backyards to explore) are on a loop that includes numbers 143, 145, 158 to 162. Midway and Fairway are more typical campgrounds. Of the electrical sites (found largely in Fairway) the best are 315, 316, 317 and 287, 289 and 290 and 294. All of these sites have good access to the beach and boat docking.

Another 100 sites are in secluded Hardwood Hills Campground. The campsites here have access to fewer facilities (they do have a comfort station), but campers relish a deliciously quiet atmosphere and plenty of wildlife, though that includes more mosquitoes. The campsites are very large and widely spaced apart, and some are suitable for tents only. Hardwood Hills is a voluntary radio-free zone. In addition to the hiking sites on the Abes and Essens Trail, there are five walk-in sites close to the conveniences of the Mazinaw Lake Campground, but with the advantage of spectacular lakeside views and few neighbours.

For visitors who would like roofed accommodation, the "Cabin on the Hill" accommodates up to six people and is rented for a week at a time during the summer. Rates are very competitive, especially during the shoulder seasons.

Local Attractions

Bon Echo Provincial Park is a long drive from many tourist attractions. It's best to plan a Bon Echo trip around outdoors activities in the park.

Fast Facts

Campgrounds: 530 sites in four campgrounds including five walk-in sites; (132 sites with hydro hookups); some sites wheelchair accessible; 30 backcountry sites. Group camping. Six-person cabin available. Comfort stations with showers, laundry, flush toilets (all accessible). Camping season mid-May to mid-October. Reservations recommended for all sites, all season long.

Supplies: Firewood is sold in the park. There is some shopping in
 Cloyne (10 km) and Kaladar (30 km).
Facilities:
 Trailer sanitation station
 Boat launches and docking
 Canoe rentals
 Ferry service to Mazinaw Rock
 Boat tours
 Beaches
 Visitor centre
 Book/gift store
 Hiking trails (five trails totalling 26 km; overnight trails
 totalling 17 km)
 Sunday church services
Winter Use: The park is closed in winter.
Contact Information: R.R. 1, Cloyne ON, K0H 1K0 tel 613-336-2228

Sandbanks Provincial Park

**Location: About 40 km south of Belleville on Lake Ontario. Access
 from Road 12.**
Natural Environment: 2   Activities: 2   Campground: 1

When the dog days of summer have you yearning for a reviving breeze
and the lulling rhythm of wavelets on sand, then head for Sandbanks
Provincial Park, one of the province's premier "destination parks." Sandbanks has two gloriously long strands of deep, white sand, and the water
is warm and shallow for a considerable distance from shore. Sandbanks
is the site of the world's largest freshwater sand-dune system—some
dunes are up to 25 m in height—which provides for memorable hiking.
The park is located in peaceful, pastoral Prince Edward County, which
beckons to daytrippers with exceptional art and antique shops, farm-gate
markets, and historic villages settled by United Empire Loyalists.

Natural Environment and History

Sandbanks is a long, narrow park located on the windward side of Prince
Edward County, where wind-deposited sands accumulate into precipitous dunes that range in height from 15 to 25 m. The park actually

encompasses two distinct dune and sandbar areas and the intervening rural lands. Early settlers originally removed the protective forest cover on the leeward side of the dunes, and the sand began a march inland, covering farms and forests in their path. Stabilization programs initiated in the 1920s and completed during the 1960s halted the sandy invasion, and the beaches of Sandbanks now resemble their earlier structure. Lake Ontario, too, deposits sand here, in the form of sandbars that are a delight to waders. The baymouth sandbar near the mouth of the Outlet River is one of the largest such bars in the world.

Sandbank's dunes support species uniquely adapted to surviving in arid soils that are continually dried by winds. Most talked-about is the wolf spider, a hairy cousin of the tarantula that stalks insects on the beach at night (and represents no danger to people). Sandbanks is the place to focus your binoculars on a rich variety of shore and water birds: several species of gulls, terns, sandpipers, plovers and ducks make their home here, and dozens more are observed during spring and fall migration. Another resident of the park is the uncommon silver-haired bat. Springtime brings botanists who study the wildflowers that thrive in the park, among them brook lobelia orchid, hoary puccoon, sea rocket and sand spurge.

Away from the beach are several different forest types, such as juniper heath, maple-beech and white cedar forest. Some of these habitats can be seen along the Cedar Dunes Trail.

Special Activities

Sandbanks Provincial Park is the place to enjoy every conceivable water toy. Boats, canoes and sailboats are used far out on the waves, and the park has two boat launches.

Swimmers have two magnificent beaches to choose from, Outlet Beach and Sandbanks Beach; the latter is the less crowded of the two but Outlet Beach is closer to the food concession in the park store. Each beach has parking lots, change rooms and washrooms. The tiny and infrequently used beach on quiet West Lake has a steep drop-off.

Conditions for windsurfing here are as good as they get in Ontario, and equipment rentals are available near the park. The watersport concession in the park rents canoes, paddleboats, kayaks and unusual "water bikes," which are bikes fastened atop surfboards and equipped with propellers and rudders.

Cedar Sands is the only trail in Sandbanks; this is a 1.5-km walk through several habitat types. To protect the fragile dune environment from trampling, staircases and boardwalks lead to a lookout over the Outlet River. Visitors can also hike the steep dunes, passing through arid juniper heath and tough dune grass to achieve the pinnacle of these sand mountains and a dramatic view of shimmering West Lake. When evening falls, there is a deep sense of serenity here, made even more satisfying by flittering bats and the barking foxes. This is one of Southern Ontario's best hikes.

A fishing spot is available to suit every taste at Sandbanks. Lovers of wide-open water hunt for chinook salmon on Lake Ontario and for big pickerel in the nearby Bay of Quinte. East and West Lakes provide angling for bass, pickerel and pike.

Park staff keep a busy schedule, with weekly campfires, guided hikes, slide shows and films. Many of these take place during the evening. Specially geared to children are hikes, games, crafts, stories and puzzles. Annual special events include a Mother's Day wildflower walk, a midsummer spirit walk and theatre in the park (a full drama presentation on local history), and autumn hikes and fun runs.

The visitor centre has displays on Sandbank's unique flora and fauna. This is also the place to find out about special events and to purchase souvenirs and nature-oriented books and toys.

Campground

Sandbanks is a very popular park, and reservations are recommended for its 547 campsites. The camping here is rather more densely packed than in other parks; often you need to make a choice between convenient beach access and campsite privacy. The Outlet River Campground is closest to the main beach and can be quite busy; sites 84 though 86, however, are secluded gems. The following sites have the best beach access in the park, but they are not very private: 18, 20, 21, 23, 24, 26, 28, 30, 32, 33, 35, 37 and 38. Cedars Campground is also close to Outlet Beach and the visitor centre; sites 321 to 328 have the most desirable combination of beach access and privacy. Woodland Campground has 140 electrical sites for trailers; 668 to 682 are the best field-situated sites and 644 to 656 and 663 to 667 are preferred treed sites. Richardson's Campground is closest to quieter Sandbanks beach and to the best dunes hiking.

For those who prefer comfort with their parks, Sandbanks rents a "summer lodge," which is a cottage that sleeps six and has all kitchen and linen necessities. The cottage has a minimum rental of a week during the summer and a two-night minimum during the off-season. (Rental rates are very competitive.)

Local Attractions

Prince Edward County is chock-full of things to see and do—a daytripper's paradise. Many historical museums celebrate the United Empire Loyalists who first settled "The County." Two examples are the Macauley Heritage Park in Picton (church, home and carriage house and gardens), and the Ameliasburg Village (pioneer village with many buildings, costumed staff and special events). Picton is also the home of the Regent Theatre, a newly restored centre for live performances of drama and music. Farm-gate markets are everywhere in this productive agricultural area, and a favourite stop for many is Black River Cheese near Picton. Prince Edward County has many delightful country towns, each one boasting historic buildings, antique shops and art studios; Wellington, Cherry Valley, Bloomfield and Milford are all well worth a visit.

Fast Facts

Campgrounds: 547 sites in four campgrounds (140 sites with hydro hookups); some wheelchair-accessible campsites. Group camping. Comfort stations with showers and flush toilets (wheelchair accessible) and laundries. Camping season early April to late October. Reservations recommended for all sites all season long.

Supplies: Firewood and ice sold in park. Food concession. Park store sells some groceries and convenience items. Best grocery shopping is in any of the towns located near the park.

Facilities:
Trailer sanitation station
Boat launches but no docking
Beaches
Visitor centre
Hiking trails (one short trail; off-trail hiking on the dunes)
Church services

Winter Use: The park is open for cross-country skiing and snowshoeing. Unserviced winter camping.

Contact Information: RR 1, Picton ON, K0K 2T0 tel 613-969-8368

Charleston Lake Provincial Park

Location: About 25 km northeast of Gananoque
near the hamlet of Outlet.

Natural Environment: 2　　　Activities: 2　　　Campground: 2

Every Ontarian's favourite backdrop for family holidays is the wild country known as the Canadian Shield. How fortunate it is that this magical mix of granite, pine and fresh air lies in such close proximity to Ottawa, Kingston and other cities of Eastern Ontario. Charleston Lake Provincial Park is 2,400 hectares of sparkling lakes and hilly, trails to explore—a true "northern" refuge located in Southern Ontario. Excellent programming and good campsites make for an outdoors holiday suitable for families and adventurers of all skill levels.

Natural Environment and History

The famous Frontenac Axis forms a geologic "bridge" between the Canadian Shield of Northern Ontario with its equivalent south of the border, the Adirondack Mountains of New York State. The park is particularly interesting to geologists for the variety of rock type found here. In addition, there is an unusual juxtaposition of sandstone that dates to 570 million years ago with Precambrian granite that is 2.5 billion years old. Where the rock from the intervening millions of years has gone remains a geologic mystery.

Charleston Lake is a diverse combination of northern forest and wildlife with the plants and animals of the more temperate St. Lawrence Lowlands. The park has many examples of northern species such as the white pine living in close quarters with southerners such as pitch pine. Because of the shallow soils and exposed rock (95 percent of the park is rock), the park has several marshes and bogs that support unique assemblages of plants and animals uncommon in other landscapes.

The rich forest and lakes here support a wide variety of wildlife, which in turn attracted a variety of human populations over the centuries. Archaeological evidence suggests use by nomadic groups of aboriginal peoples; in fact, the park has over 30 prehistoric sites where pottery and other artifacts were uncovered. These relics are on display in the park visitor centre.

Later in history, Charleston Lake became a tourist centre and cottages dotted the shoreline. The era of the steamboat brought pleasure cruisers from across Ontario and New York, and the lake became a busy place indeed. Although few physical remnants of the cottages or the steamships remain, that era of elegance is often recalled during park historical skits.

Special Activities

Charleston Lake is a perfect park for exploration by water or by foot. Indeed, you would be hard pressed to find better hiking in Eastern Ontario. Six trails vary in length from 1.6 km to 14 km. Family hiking is available along the 2.6-km Quiddity Trail that leads to a lookout over beautiful Running's Bay. Two boardwalks on this trail provide about 0.5 km of barrier-free hiking. The Westside Trail is a 14-km return trip through the park's least-travelled forest. Wildlife viewing is excellent along the Beech Woods Trail (1.8 km) and the Hemlock Ridge Trail (1.8 km). Sandstone Island Trail (3.3 km) brings hikers to the picturesque site of an ancient firepit sheltered by an overhanging cliff. Not only were aboriginal artifacts found at this site, but also gunflint and musket balls from later European travellers. Excellent interpretive brochures on these latter three trails are available at the trail start-points. Long-distance trekkers may use the 13 interior campsites.

Paddling is excellent on Charleston Lake, which has many scenic islands and shimmering bays. The park provides canoe rentals at each of its two beaches. Beginning paddlers appreciate the motorboat-free conditions in Running's Bay and Slim Bay. Boating, sailing and fishing for lake trout and bass are popular pastimes here as well. Facilities include a boat launch and a dock.

Charleston Lake's interpretive program operates several times daily all summer long. Guided hikes by foot and canoe are frequently offered, as are historical skits, storytimes and Saturday-night campfires with entertainment. The children's program is particularly rich, with activities aimed at three separate age groups: 1 to 5 years, 6 to 10 years, and 11 to 16 years. The visitor centre has displays on local history and ecology and is open all summer.

Charleston Lake is very popular during the winter, and the park's pristine and deeply peaceful beauty is appreciated by photographers. Skiing and snowshoeing are enjoyed under snow-laden boughs, though there are no officially maintained trails. Overnight camping is also available by prior arrangement with park staff.

Campground

There are 236 campsites at Charleston Lake, 83 of these with hydro hookup. Each of the three campgrounds has a comfort station with showers, flush toilets and laundry. The Meadowlands Campground has sites that are very open to the road, but have good privacy from adjacent campsites. The best sites here are numbers 112, 113 and 119. The Bayside Campground has several sites close to Running's Bay; sites 230 and 238 are especially good. The Shady Ridge Campground has the greatest number of recommended campsites: numbers 303, 304 to 310 (even numbers), 335, 340 and 341 (closest to the water), and sites 343 and 358.

Local Attractions

Charleston Lake is centrally located in an idyllic backwater of historic limestone villages, antique shops and pastoral scenery. Nearby Athens is well known for the huge murals that decorate buildings throughout town. A self-guiding brochure is available from downtown merchants. The country roads around Athens have many excellent antique shops to explore. Lyndhurst, Delta, Crosby and Portland are also pleasant villages. Delta's five-storey stone mill is especially photogenic, and Portland has a waterfront that invites a stroll. Merrickville is one of Ontario's prettiest and most photographed towns, and for good reason. With a museum, a fascinating historic site, many dining places and dozens of studios and shops, Merrickville can easily fill a very pleasant day.

Fast Facts

Campgrounds: 236 sites in three campgrounds (83 sites have hydro hookups); some sites are wheelchair accessible. Group camping; 13 backcountry sites. Comfort stations with showers, laundry, flush toilets. Camping season is from mid-May to late October. Reservations recommended for all sites, all season long.

Supplies: Firewood sold in the park. Groceries available in Lyndhurst or Lansdowne (each about 10 km).

Facilities:
Trailer sanitation station
Seasonal storage of trailers/boats
Boat launch and docking
Canoe rentals and canoe storage
Beach
Visitor centre
Hiking trail (six trails totalling over 30 km, some sections wheelchair accessible)

Winter Use: Park open all winter; cross-country ski trails and ski events.

Contact Information: 148 Woodvale Road, Lansdowne ON, K0E 1L0
tel 613-659-2065

Parks of the St. Lawrence

**Location: Along the St. Lawrence River between Cornwall
and Gananoque. Access from Long Sault Parkway and
1000 Islands Parkway.**

Natural Environment: 1   Activities: 2   Campground: 1

Ontario's St. Lawrence River shoreline is the stuff daydreams are made of:
a broad river dotted with thousands of rocky islets; castles and forts sheltered by windswept pine; tales of tragic romance, smuggling and warfare.
The region that stretches along the St. Lawrence River from the 1000
Islands east to Cornwall has attractions enough to last an entire summer.
Just for starters, there is the 1000 Islands Parkway, the Long Sault Parkway, Upper Canada Village and Fort Wellington. Several campgrounds
and day-use parks are located along the St. Lawrence River; though they
are widely separated from one another, they are all administered under
the umbrella of the Parks of the St. Lawrence.

Natural Environment and History

The St. Lawrence Valley is made of two distinct regions: the 1000 Islands
and the St. Lawrence Seaway. The 1000 Islands is famous for its countless
small islands, each a rocky offshoot of the Precambrian Shield. Some of
the islands are tiny specks of barren land where only a few shrubs and a
pine tree can eke out a living. Other islands are forested refuges for the
rich and famous; several have summer homes lavish enough to bear the
title of "castle."

At first glance, pink rock and white pine gives the region a very
northern appearance but the presence of many southern species identifies this as a true transition zone. Naturalists come to the islands to see
pitch pine, shagbark hickory, and white and red oak grow with pin cherry
and yellow birch. Some of the islands support colonies of black-crowned
night heron, double-crested cormorant, herring gull and caspian tern.
Bald eagles are seen along the river during winter.

Downstream from the 1,000 Islands is the St. Lawrence Seaway
region. The landscape here is more rural, with areas of level farmland and
young forest. This was not always the situation. At one time, the St.
Lawrence River was a turbulent scene of treacherous whitewater—the
Long Sault Rapids. The construction of an immense hydro dam at Cornwall obliterated the rapids, which were flooded under the dam's

headpond. Entire villages and many farms were also flooded. The islands of the region are actually the hilltops of the original landscape. The forest is comprised of very young trees and shrubs that are invading abandoned agricultural land.

The St. Lawrence Seaway region is still predominantly rural. Along the river itself are several large marshes that are significant refuges for migrating waterfowl. Black duck, mallard and Canada goose breed in the marshes, and turtles, kingfisher and muskrat are common. During the winter the river attracts many water birds such as common merganser, oldsquaw, canvasback, scaup, great black-backed gull and Iceland gulls.

Special Activities

Boating is a popular activity along the St. Lawrence, and almost all the Parks of the St. Lawrence have boat launches. About 20 species of fish, from pike to pickerel, can be caught in the river. Gananoque and Brockville are the best harbours for sailing and fishing charters or boat rentals. The Grenadier Ferry picks up passengers at Mallorytown Landing and transports them to some of the 21 islands of St. Lawrence Islands National Park. The islands have beaches, picnic spots and boat launches; some islands have campsites. Brockville's civic marina is another place to hire a ferry for transport to the 27 islands owned by that city.

Several parks have beaches. One of the best is at Brown's Bay, which is actually part of St. Lawrence Islands National Park. The water here is pleasantly warm; an added attraction is an interesting museum built to protect the remains of an 1812 gunboat.

The 1000 Islands Parkway (38 km) makes a great pleasure-drive or bike-ride between Gananoque and Mallorytown Landing. Around each bend in the road is a new vista of countless tiny islands, colourful sailboats and speeding powerboats. Good driving and excellent cycling are also found along the Long Sault Parkway, which connects Long Sault with Ingleside. This ribbon of asphalt hops from island to island (preflooding hilltops), passing beaches, picnic sites and wooded hiking trails. Scuba diving to view the village and original seaway locks is a popular activity. A museum dedicated to the "Lost Villages" is located at Ault Park near the village of Long Sault.

The Upper Canada Bird Sanctuary has 8 km of hiking trails and 5 km of these trails are used during winter for cross-country skiing. There is a short trail at the St. Lawrence Islands National Park headquarters at Mallorytown Landing.

Campground

There are five campgrounds in the 1000 Islands and St. Lawrence Seaway areas. Three of these campgrounds are located along the Long Sault Parkway between Long Sault and Ingleside. The campsites at McLaren and Woodlands are rather open and lacking in privacy. Both of these campgrounds have beaches; McLaren has a boat launch. Although the campsites at Mille Roches are very open to the road, they are private from one another. The best sites here are numbers 69, 125 and 208. Mille Roches has a playground and several water-access areas that are convenient for boat launching.

Riverside-Cedars Campground is just east of Morrisburg. The campsites here are too exposed to be recommended. Site number 38 is perhaps the best of the lot. This campground also offers inexpensive, roofed accommodation in the form of small cabins complete with appliances and a waterfront setting with dockage (no trees, however). The campground has sports facilities, playground and a boat launch.

Ivy Lea Campground is in the heart of the 1000 Islands and has 83 campsites, 33 of these with electricity. The campground has a comfort station with showers, flush toilets and a laundry, a boat launch here, a tiny beach and a playground. These sites, though generally densely spaced and without great privacy, are the best campsites in the Parks of the St. Lawrence. Some several dozen open sites are suitable for large trailers, and many small wooded sites are suitable for tents. The sites with greatest privacy are numbers 96, 102, 123 and 124. If you telephone to reserve a campsite at Ivy Lea, try to avoid one of the sites directly underneath the heavily travelled Ivy Lea Bridge (numbers 71 and 72).

Local Attractions

No trip to the 1000 Islands is complete without a boat cruise. The largest boats depart from Gananoque; there are also cruises from Rockport, a village situated in the heart of the islands.

The 1000 Islands–Long Sault region has dozens of noteworthy attractions. Upper Canada Village near Morrisburg is 27 hectares of buildings, waterways, a mill and two working farms that represent a St. Lawrence River community during the mid-19th century. Costumed interpreters play the roles of villagers to perfection. There are two restaurants on site as well as a good gift shop. Another site well worth a visit is opulent Fulford Place in Brockville. With over 8,000 furnishings and lavish decoration, Fulford Place is a showcase of the best in Edwardian elegance.

Prescott is home to Fort Wellington, every child's dream of a barricaded fort. Guided tours and military re-enactments take place during the summer. Just a short walk away from the fort is the Stockade Barracks and Hospital Museum. This Georgian home dates to 1820 and saw action as a military barracks and hospital for soldiers serving at Fort Wellington. The tours here are a fascinating description of medical and military conditions on Upper Canada's frontier.

One of the best places to appreciate nature's beauty is at the Gardens at Landon Bay. This privately owned facility has nature trails through woodland managed for wildlife habitat, dozens of specialty gardens (from herb gardens to a butterfly haven), and many nature-oriented events year-round. The Gardens at Landon Bay are on the 1000 Islands Parkway just east of Gananoque.

Excellent wildlife-viewing opportunities exist at the Upper Canada Bird Sanctuary just east of Upper Canada Village. Nine thousand hectares of marsh and field are home to 2,000 Canada geese, but is more important as a rest stop for thousands of migrating geese and ducks. Guided nature walks take place here in the summer, and from mid-September to mid-November, a geese-feeding program provides plenty of up-close opportunities for photographs.

Fast Facts

Campgrounds: 1,086 campsites in five campgrounds (316 with hydro hookups); some sites wheelchair accessible; 9 walk-in sites. Group camping. Seasonal leasing. Comfort stations with showers, laundry, flush toilets (wheelchair accessible). Cabins available at Riverside-Cedar Campground. Camping season mid-May to early September. Reservations recommended for all sites all summer long.

Supplies: Firewood sold in the park. Some campgrounds have food concessions. Groceries best purchased in Morrisburg, Cornwall or Gananoque.

Facilities:
Trailer sanitation station
Boat launches
Beaches
Biking trails
Hiking trails

Winter Use: The parks are open all winter for walking and ungroomed cross-country skiing.

Contact Information: St. Lawrence Parks Commission, RR 1, Morrisburg ON, K0C 1X0 tel 800-437-2233

Voyageur Provincial Park

Location: About 110 km east of Ottawa on the Ottawa River.
  Close to the Quebec border.
Natural Environment: 1   Activities: 1   Campground: 2

Ontario's most easterly park, Voyageur is a popular destination for families from Ontario, Quebec and the United States who seek a relaxing place in the sun. For those who prefer big-city attractions along with their beaches and fresh air, Voyageur is conveniently close to Montreal. The park's 1,400 ha of open woods and meadows provide for good cycling and roller-blading on kilometres of level, paved road. The Ottawa River provides excellent boating and fishing, and birdwatchers gather here in spring and fall to observe large numbers of migrating waterfowl and shorebirds. Voyageur is unique among Ontario's parks in that it offers trail rides and riding lessons from a stable located close to the campgrounds.

Natural Environment and History

The Ottawa River is the most dramatic feature of the landscape. The river appears especially broad and calm here, but this belies its turbulent condition before the construction of the Carillon hydro dam (just downstream from the park) in 1964. The terrestrial part of Voyageur is on the fertile flatlands called the St. Lawrence Lowlands, a mix of open fields, hardwood forest and wetlands.

The park has wildlife typical of open meadows, such as deer and woodchucks. Wetlands support beaver, muskrat, painted and snapping turtles as well as kingfisher and osprey. Fall migration is particularly interesting here because huge numbers of duck, geese and shorebirds

congregate in the bays of the Ottawa River to rest and feed before continuing southward.

Voyageur's human history is particularly rich. The Ottawa River was
Ontario's first transportation corridor, and stories of early river men—
Champlain, fur traders and loggers—still resound through the region.
The park marks the location of treacherous rapids, and the early
voyageurs portaged around the whitewater at this very place. When the
logging boom began, a canal constructed between Voyageur and
Grenville in 1829 moved logs around the rapids. The canal also stimu-
lated farms and settlements, making this one of the first regions of
Ontario to experience significant development. Stone and split-rail
fences, relics of United Empire Loyalist farms, are seen along park trails.
The river is still the focus of life in Eastern Ontario; the 1964 Carillon
Power Dam is only the most recent use of the river for industry.

Special Activities

Swimmer appreciate Voyageur's sand beaches. The park is a very popular
with boaters and sailors. Power motors are needed to travel any distance
on the river, although small boats and canoes are a good way to explore
quiet bays and inlets. Fishing is next to boating as a pastime at Voyageur.
Pike, pickerel, bass and catfish are sought in various seasons. The park
rents boats, canoes and paddleboats and three boat launches are also
provided.

The park has two short nature trails that are suitable for young children. The Coureur de Bois Trail (3.2 km) travels through upland forests,
and past swamps and beaver ponds. This is a good place to spot heron,
turtles, woodpeckers, ducks and muskrats. The 2.5-km Outaouais Trail
connects several park beaches, playing fields (baseball and soccer), picnic areas and the park store. This trail, which will be expanded to include
the amphitheatre and park entrance, makes this a very pedestrian-
friendly park because the need to walk on park roads is eliminated.

The summer interpretive program has several events each week,
including hikes, children's activities, and evening presentations in the
amphitheatre. In October there is the annual Waterfowl Day, a perfect
opportunity to learn the differences between canvasbacks, redheads and
other ducks. The day includes guided birdwatching hikes, bird-banding
demonstrations, a scavenger hunt and an art exhibit. Interpretive services
are offered in both English and French.

During winter, skiers can take advantage of 12 km of groomed trails
suitable for beginners.

Campground

Voyageur Provincial Park has 416 campsites (110 with hydro hookups) in three campgrounds that have comfort stations with showers and flush toilets. The Portage and Champlain comfort stations have laundries. The Iroquois and Champlain Campgrounds have playgrounds.

There is much variety to choose from in the campsites at Voyageur. Even though Portage Campground has shrub and meadow growth, the most private sites are here, particularly sites 303 to 307 (electrical), 312 to 315, 318, 320, 326, 336 and 338. The sites in the Champlain Campground are generally spacious and well treed. The best sites here are on the river (boat access to sites), such as numbers 77 to 85 and 87 to 95 (all odd numbers).

The campground store sells a few groceries and also offers a fast-food concession.

Local Attractions

Voyageur's hinterland is steeped in Ontario's early history. Tiny Williamstown and its excellent Nor'Westers and Loyalist Museum is the spot to pay tribute to the tough-minded Scots fur-traders who explored a continent. Thompson House in Williamstown is Ontario's oldest house (1784), and the village hosts Ontario's oldest fall fair (begun in 1808). Nearby Maxville is the place to be in August, the month for the town's fabulous Highland Games, well known internationally for competition in dance and athletics. St. Raphael's was an enormous 1815 stone church gutted by fire in 1970; the ruins are a distinctly romantic sight.

Voyageur is well situated for exploring the Quebec side of the Ottawa River. Cross the river by way of the bridge at Hawkesbury or by taking the delightful and efficient ferry at Lefaivre. The ferry arrives at the village of Montebello, where everyone should at least visit the grounds and enjoy a fine meal at Canadian Pacific's enchanting Chateau Montebello. The extensive grounds include the historic Manoir Papineau, a sumptuously furnished home for Louis-Joseph Papineau, leader in Quebec politics in the early 1800s.

Fast Facts

Campgrounds: 416 sites in three campgrounds (110 sites with hydro hookups); some sites wheelchair accessible. Group camping. Seasonal leasing. Comfort stations with showers, laundry, flush toilets (wheelchair accessible). Camping season mid-May to mid-October. Reservations recommended for all sites from June to mid-August and on all long weekends.

Supplies: Firewood and ice sold in park. Park store sells some groceries and light meals. Shopping available in Chute-a-Blondeau (5 km) and in Hawkesbury (14 km).

Facilities:
Trailer sanitation station
Trailer/boat storage
Boat launches
Canoe and boat rentals
Beaches
Playground
Horseback riding
Hiking trails (two trails totalling 5 km)

Winter Use: The park has groomed cross-country ski trails for all levels of skier.

Contact Information: Box 130, Chute-à-Blondeau ON, K0B 1B0
tel 613-674-2825

Vacancy

144

SUDBURY

LAKE NIPISSING

NORTH BAY

Ottawa River

36

34

33

11

30

17

OTTAWA

417

35

GEORGIAN BAY

69

31

60

41

CORNWALL

15

32

401

St. Lawrence River

6

37

35

26

OWEN SOUND

BARRIE

LAKE SIMCOE

7

PETERBOROUGH

KINGSTON

BELLEVILLE

11

21

6

400

7

TORONTO

LAKE ONTARIO

HAMILTON

401

QEW

NIAGARA FALLS

LONDON

CENTRAL ONTARIO

LEGEND

30 Algonquin Provincial Park
31 Arrowhead Provincial Park
32 Silent Lake Provincial Park
33 Restoule Provincial Park
34 Killarney Provincial Park
35 Killbear Provincial Park
36 Grundy Lake Provincial Park
37 Awenda Provincial Park

Central Ontario

Algonquin Provincial Park

Location: In Central Ontario between Ottawa and North Bay. Most campgrounds and facilities are located along Highway 60.

Natural Environment: 3   Activities: 3   Campground: 2

Algonquin Provincial Park is so expansive—larger than some countries—and offers such a tantalizing array of year-round outdoors experiences that it is justifiably the subject of dozens of publications. Although Algonquin's canoe trips in the park are the stuff summers are made of, there are countless "soft adventures" to be had closer at hand and demanding less athleticism. Activities undertaken individually or with the assistance of local outfitters include mountain biking, hiking, canoeing, kayaking, dog-sledding, cross-country skiing, snowshoeing and winter camping. The outstanding visitor centre has award-winning dioramas and other exhibits that highlight the park's history and natural features. Park staff conduct programs daily, including canoe "hikes," movies, lectures, and of course, the famous August wolf howls.

Natural Environment and History

While most other parks are measured in hectares, Algonquin is measured in square kilometres—7,725 of them—which is too much natural splendour to consume at one gulp. The park's most striking feature is its hills, which rise in every direction, covered with mixed forest of maple, aspen, oak, birch and majestic white pine. While much of the park is secondary growth (after fires and logging removed the virgin timber), you can find places where original white pine and red pine are over 350 years in age and 35 metres in height. Photogenic in all seasons, Algonquin's vast forests are breathtaking in autumn, when each species contributes to the mosaic of plum, orange, scarlet and gold. Many of the hills are crested with barren rocks, cliffs and ridges. In the deep valleys are wetland communities: rivers, lakes (some with sandy beaches), open marsh or black spruce meadows.

Most visitors come to Algonquin with hope of seeing wildlife, and few people leave disappointed. Moose are so common here that they are almost a park symbol, and photographers often capture a huge moose, its head dripping with water and raised to watch a canoe passing by. Moose are most likely to be seen at dawn or dusk, with May and June being the best viewing months. Loons, too, are near the top of the popularity list, and are seen on most lakes. Other wildlife in Algonquin are beaver, river otter, bear and porcupine. The elusive marten and fisher are seen less frequently, though the park is well known as an important refuge for these fur-bearers. Algonquin is a feast for birdwatchers, with over 250 species on the park bird checklist. That list includes gray jay, raven and spruce grouse.

Special Activities

For many Ontarians, Algonquin is synonymous with canoe tripping—that could be because of its 1,500 canoe routes. There are, however, plenty of single-day excursions that can provide solitude and rejuvenation in a backwoods environment. Ask at the visitor centre for suggestions. Canoes and any other equipment may be rented from outfitters within the park; delivery of gear to your campsite or to your entry point can be arranged. In order to preserve Algonquin's natural calm, motorboats (up to 20 horsepower) are permitted only on a few lakes, and waterskiing and jet skiing are prohibited.

Hiking Algonquin's hills is made perfectly enjoyable through an extensive network of trails. Pick up a self-guiding brochure for each trail at the park entrance or at the visitor centre. Long distance hikers head for the Highland, Western Uplands or Eastern Pines trails that range from 6 to 88 km in length and that have campsites en route. The park also has 16 day-hike trails varying from 0.8 to 11 km in length. One of the most popular trails for wildlife viewing is the Mizzy Lake Trail, an 11-km loop that traverses nine ponds and lakes (no dogs allowed). The Lookout Trail is a 0.9-km trip to a rocky summit with a commanding view of lakes and forest. Demanding Centennial Ridges Trail is a 10-km hike with cliff-hugging sections and scenic lookouts. For less strenuous outings, try the 1.5-km Spruce Bog Boardwalk or the 2-km Beaver Pond Trail.

Perhaps the best trail of them all is on the eastern end the park, accessible from Achray Road. A 1.5-km path leads to a breathtaking view high on the cliffs over the Barron River Canyon. This is one of Ontario's most spectacular settings: sheer rock walls tower over the placid river far below. Even in midsummer you could well be entirely alone with the wind, the ravens and the river. In winter this is a good place to see wolves and eagles.

Cyclists have two choices for off-road excursions. The 10-km Old Railway Bike Trail connects the Mew Lake and Rock Lake Campgrounds and follows the abandoned route of the Ottawa, Arnprior and Parry Sound Railway. The trail is level and ideal for family cycling. Mountain bikers head for the Minnesing Trail, a hilly, forested adventure for two wheels; the trail has four loops ranging from 4.7 to 23 km in length.

Many of the lakes in the Highway 60 corridor are stocked with splake for almost guaranteed good fishing, and numerous interior lakes have lake trout, best sought in early spring. Bass fishing is popular in many lakes near to the campgrounds.

No visitor should leave Algonquin without a half-day spent at the extraordinary visitor centre. This is the place to tap the knowledge of park staff to plan canoe or hiking trips into the interior, and check the wildlife-sightings board (updated almost hourly) to find the latest wildlife news. The centre is most famous for its dioramas—lifelike depictions of daily life in various park habitats. From a loon in pursuit of silvery, darting fish to a deer mouse evading detection by a predator, each scene is artistically and factually accurate. Children enjoy the many interactive exhibits, such as an animated logger and computer quizzes based on life in the park. An excellent multimedia show covers the natural and human history of the park, including the role of fire and logging in changing the natural environment forever. The centre's balcony is high over a meandering stream and pond; and when a tiny red canoe with life-jacketed paddlers passes by far below, all observers sigh wistfully.

Algonquin's visitor program has many elements; often three or four activities are going on at once! Conducted walks take place mornings, afternoons and evenings, and some of these are designated for children. Evening programs also include films and slide shows. Canoe hikes, lessons and demonstrations are conducted by staff and by the Ontario Recreational Canoe Association. The visitor centre organizes a "paint-out" with visiting artists, so that campers can accompany professional artists as they capture the park on canvas. The famous wolf howls (Thursdays in August) are when staff attempt to locate wolf packs and entice the young wolves to howl, an experience everyone will remember.

The Algonquin Logging Museum is located near the eastern end of the Highway 60 corridor. Outdoor exhibits and several buildings explore the technology of logging in the park (horses were used as recently as the 1950s) and the lifestyle of the tough-spirited individuals carrying on the trade. There is also an audio-visual program. Highlights include the steam-powered "alligator" used to haul log booms across the water.

Algonquin is increasingly popular for winter activities. Winter camping (Mew Lake Campground), snowshoeing, cross-country skiing (80 km of trails in loops of 5 to 42 km) and ice fishing all take place in the park.

Campgrounds

Not surprisingly, with over 7,000 square km of space and great popular demand for camping, Algonquin's park planners have developed many different campgrounds. Over 1,200 spaces are available in conventional campgrounds, as well as over 1,900 sites on remote lakes accessible only by foot or by paddle. This following is a brief summary of the campgrounds in the Highway 60 corridor.

Tea Lake: 42 sites, most very open and close to Highway 60, making Tea Lake one of the least desirable campgrounds. There is no comfort station, here but there is a boat launch and small beach. Number 30 is a nice walk in-site, and number 42 is more private than the others. Sites 10 to 14 have views of the lake.

Canisbay Lake: 242 sites (67 with electrical hookups) and 16 paddle-in sites (by reservation only). Canisbay has good beaches and comfort stations. The Minnesing Mountain Bike Trail is easily accessed from this campground. Most electrical sites at Canisbay tend to be small and closely spaced. The best non-electrical sites are numbers 1 to 10, 20 to 27, 30, 32 and 41 (many of these are suitable for tents only and are among the best sites in Algonquin). The campsite loops numbered 102 to 242 are more open but are also more spacious and are best suited for trailers. Good sites here are numbers 154, 163 and 171, 173, 175, 228 to 230. Sites 53 to 101 are in a radio- and dog-free zone.

Mew Lake: 131 sites (66 electrical), some sites in open fields and some in forest. The campground has a beach and comfort station. There is excellent access to Old Railway Bike Path, the Lake of Two Rivers store (convenience items and ice cream) and the Track & Tower Trail. The open sites (1 to 66) are closest to the beach and are electrical; they are rather closely spaced. In the radio- and dog-free zone, the best sites are 100, 102, 104, 128 and 129. Other sites at Mew Lake are rather too close to Highway 60. The campground has three "yurts" available for rent.

Lake of Two Rivers: 241 sites, many of them with electrical hookup, are situated in white pine forest. This campground has Algonquin's largest beach and a shoreline spot for beaching boats. The Two Rivers

Store is adjacent to the campground. Highway noise may be a problem for sites closest to the Highway 60. The electrical sites at Lake of Two Rivers have more large trees than similar sites elsewhere in the park, however, there is a little undergrowth for visual privacy.

Pog Lake: 286 campsites (81 with electric hookups). This campground has several comfort stations and two beaches. Some of the campsites at Pog Lake are the best in the park, and are highly recommended. Section A, the dog- and radio-free zone, is rather close to busy Highway 60, but has some nice sites (201, 209, 216 to 22 and 221 and 222). Electrical sites are in Campground B and are closest to the large beach. Campground C is by far the best area, especially sites 424 and 435, which are on quiet loops. Site 460 is a large site for those who require space, but is quite open.

Kearney Lake: 103 unserviced sites with a comfort station but no laundry. Although no motorboats are permitted, the campground has a small beach. The sites here are spaced farther apart than in many other campgrounds. Kearney Lake has good access to the Old Railway Bike Trail.

Coon Lake: 49 unserviced sites with no comfort station. There is a little privacy at Coon Lake and the sites tend to be small, but campers enjoy good access to the Centennial Ridges Trail and the Old Railway Bike Trail. This campground is one of two located well away from Highway 60.

Rock Lake: 119 sites (71 with hydro) in a campground with a boat launch and a comfort station. Rock Lake is well off Highway 60. The electrical campsites are close to a beach, but are rather closely spaced together under pine trees. Of the non-hydro sites (also with their own beach), sites 73 to 76 provide good lakes views and maximum privacy. Sites 104 to 106 are also recommended.

There are campgrounds at the north end of the park (Kiosk has 17 sites and Brent has 30 sites) and at the Achray or eastern end of the park (39 sites). These simple campgrounds have beaches, but are without showers. The Brent campground has a store and the Achray and Kiosk campgrounds have docks; all three campgrounds have boat launches.

Another option for accommodation is eleven ranger cabins that date back almost a century and which are located in remote but beautiful backcountry. The cabins are heated and some are available for winter camping; some have electricity and others have propane fridges. The cabins vary in size, accommodating from four to eight people. While some cabins are for walk-in visitors, the Kiosk Campground and the Rain Lake entrance both have cabins that are accessible by car.

Local Attractions

One could spend summer after summer camping in Algonquin and not exhaust all the outdoor recreation possibilities. This is increasingly true as private outfitters increase their presence in the park, offering easy canoe rental and delivery facilities, and lead day-long and extended excursions into the park.

For those determined to travel outside the park for activity, there are some interesting options. To the southwest, Haliburton has an historic museum and art gallery, as well as holiday shopping and restaurants. To the southeast of Algonquin lie many possibilities, such as white water kayaking and rafting (family level) at Barry's Bay. Further away, Wilno has an outstanding art store and a restaurant of large renown.

Fast Facts

Campgrounds: 1,327 sites in 11 campgrounds (447 with hydro hookups); some sites wheelchair accessible; 1,946 backcountry sites. Group campsites. Seasonal leasing only at Achray Campground. Yurts available at Achray and Mew Lake Campgrounds. Backcountry cabins available. Many campgrounds have comfort stations with showers, laundry, flush toilets (often laundries are not accessible). Camping season for most campgrounds from early April to mid-October. Reservations recommended for all sites, all season long.

Supplies: Firewood, ice, some groceries and ice-cream stand at Lake of Two Rivers camp store. Better shopping in Whitney (about 5 km and in Dorset (about 15 km).

Facilities:
Trailer sanitation station
Boat launches
Canoe rentals
Visitor centre with cafeteria
Art gallery
Beaches
Bike path (one path totalling 10 km)
Mountain biking trails (four loops totalling 5, 10, 17 and 23 km)
Hiking trails (16 trails totalling 64 km; overnight trails totalling 138 km)

Winter Use: The park is open all winter and has extensive cross-country trails. Winter camping available.

Contact Information: Box 219, Whitney ON, K0J 2M0
tel 705-633-5572

Arrowhead Provincial Park

Location: 3 km north of Huntsville on Highway 11.
Natural Environment: 3   **Activities:** 2   **Campground:** 2

Central Ontario's cottage country is often labelled our "four-season play-ground," so it's appropriate that the region's largest park, Arrowhead, offers outdoor pleasure throughout the year. Summertime hiking at Arrowhead takes place on several trails. The Big East River provides canoeing for all skill levels. Park staff are just as committed to showing winter visitors an excellent time, with Ontario's most extraordinary toboggan experience, skating, and trails for cross-country skiing, snow-shoeing and walking. The large campground is well laid out and is accessible by a forested entrance road long enough to keep the camp-ground well separated from Highway 11.

Natural Environment and History

Nature has blessed Arrowhead with many riches, such as hills covered with a lovely forest of Muskoka hardwoods. Maple, yellow and white birch, hemlock and pine form a pretty combination at any time, but especially in autumn when the colour display in the park is spectacular. In level areas of the park such as the campground, a younger forest of aspen and birch predominates. Birds and mammals typical of mature forest are commonly seen and heard, among them warblers, thrushes, flycatchers, chipmunks and squirrels.

The park has two lakes, tiny Mayflower and Arrowhead, the latter named for the aquatic plant that grows in the lake's shallows. The Big East River meanders through the park through a broad valley with high sandy banks originally carved by a much larger glacial waterway. Ice ages left behind the sand beaches on Arrowhead Lake and the gravely ridges that mark glacial lakeshores. The park's scenic highlight is Stubb's Falls, where the Little East River tumbles and cascades over boulders in a scene that is equally attractive in all seasons.

Special Activities

There's plenty to do at Arrowhead. Three short hiking trails are enjoyable and easy walking. The Homesteader's Trail is the longest at 3 km and takes in a bog and all that remains of a homesteader's hard work: a stone foundation, rhubarb plants and rusting equipment. The Mayflower Lake

Trail (one kilometre) is short but hilly, and circles the spring-fed lake that is home to many kinds of snakes and frogs. Stubb's Falls Trail is a favourite haunt in both summer and winter. A short pathway leads from the Roe Campground to a scenic view of the Big East River.

Canoe launches are situated on both Mayflower and Arrowhead Lakes and canoe rentals are available. The lakes are fished for speckled trout and bass, and visitors ice-fish for trout each winter. Arrowhead Lake's three sandy beaches on Arrowhead Lake are popular for sunbathing and waterplay.

Canoeists love Arrowhead, for both the Little East and the Big East River have kilometres of portage-free canoeing. Although best known as a route for novice and intermediate skill levels, there are some challenging sections for experienced paddlers. A map and description of canoe routes in the park is available from park staff. Arrowhead and Mayflower Lakes are also popular for canoeing.

The visitor centre is the place to find out about the events scheduled five days a week; the possibilities include movie nights, guided hikes, spirit walks and guests speakers.

Of all Ontario's parks, Arrowhead has the best facilities and programming for wintertime fun. There's ice fishing and skating on the frozen lakes. Cross-country skiers, both traditionalists and skate-skiers, travel along 27 km of groomed trails. Walkers and snowshoers have their own trail to Stubb's Falls so that bootprints don't spoil the quality of the ski trails. The park offers ski rentals and a warm-up hut.

Total exhilaration is guaranteed when you test your courage on Arrowhead's outstanding toboggan run. A section of steep campground roadway is groomed and iced to create a run with high banks on one side and a walkway for returning uphill on the other side. You choose a very rapid descent on long plastic strips or a slightly more sedate and comfortable ride on a huge inner-tube (equipment supplied by the park). On weekends a concession stand is open; otherwise, outdoor barbecues are popular for preparing hot snacks.

Campgrounds

There are three campgrounds with total of 388 campsites (115 of these with electricity). Roe and East River campgrounds are especially well planned, with many roads ending in cul-de-sacs that minimize traffic levels. Although campers in higher numbered sites in the East River Campground (sites 322 to 351) are close to Stubb's Falls, they are far from the beach. However, these are among the nicest sites in the park. Roe Campground has its own small beach and almost all sites in Rowe are private and spacious. Sites 490 to 501 are recommended. Lumby Campground tends to be more densely spaced. Lumby has its own beach and sites closest to the beach include numbers 159 to 170.

Comfort stations in each campground have showers and flush toilets. The park store sells firewood, ice and basic groceries.

Local Attractions

The Muskoka Pioneer Village is worth a half-day's visit. Fourteen furnished buildings—homes, a church, temperance hall, and a general store—portray life in a Muskoka village of the 19th century. Special events such as a strawberry social are held throughout the summer.

One of the region's most unusual sites is the Dyer Memorial, a stone pylon erected by Dyer in memory of his wife; the couple honeymooned in Muskoka 20 years earlier. The memorial stands among groomed gardens that make a dramatic contrast to the forested surroundings. The memorial is on the north side of the Big East River, and is about 11 km from the town of Huntsville. Park staff will be able to provide directions.

Fast Facts

Campgrounds: 388 sites in three campgrounds (115 with hydro hookups); some sites wheelchair accessible. Comfort stations with showers and flush toilets (accessible). Camping season from mid-May to mid-October. Reservations recommended all sites on long weekends and during mid-July to mid-August.

Supplies: Basic groceries, ice and firewood are sold at the park store. Better shopping is in Huntsville (3 km).

Facilities:
Trailer sanitation station
Canoe launch but no docking
Canoe rentals
Beaches
Hiking trails (three trails totaling 6 km)

Winter Use: Mid-December to late March. Toboganning, ice-fishing, cross-country skiing, walking and snowshoeing. Warm-up huts, ski rentals, free tobogganing supplies.

Contact Information: R.R. 3, Huntsville ON, P1H 2J4 tel 705-789-5105

Silent Lake Provincial Park

Location: 25 km south of Bancroft on Highway 28.
Natural Environment: 2   Activities: 3   Campground: 3

Silent Lake Provincial Park is a gem waiting to be discovered, a pristine landscape with a far-north feel located close enough to our southern cities for weekend trips. Silent Lake has changed little since the region around Bancroft was first settled, protected as it was from development by early purchase as a lodge. Modern-day park managers wisely pursue such policies as a ban on motorboats and snowmobiles to ensure Silent Lake's continued tranquillity. When on the park's excellent trails to ski, hike or cycle into the bush, it is easy to imagine that this is your own little piece of Canadian Shield.

Natural Environment and History

Silent Lake offers 1,420 hectares of uninterrupted, classic Ontario scenery sure to tug at the heart: sparkling pink granite, pine-sheltered shorelines, beaver ponds and hilltop lookouts. The park's rocky hills, called by some the "backbone of the earth," are part of the region's legendary rockhounding country, and the bedrock in the park is among the most mineral-rich rock in the world. Quartz and amethyst are among the minerals commonplace here. (No sampling is permitted within the park itself, however).

Although at first glance the park is all northern forest, it actually lies in a diverse transition zone between north and south. The forest is a mix of white pine and hemlock, maple and birch. Likewise, the animal population is diverse. Southerners scarlet tanager and brown thrasher nest here along with northerners gray jay and raven. Mammals living in the park include bear, moose, deer, mink and otter.

Sections of the park are recovering from logging and forest fire. Open, sunny meadows are quickly rejuvenating as havens for wildflowers that grow in profusion. Silent Lake's interest for botanists includes several rare flowers such as rose pogonia, rattlesnake fern and toothwort.

Special Activities

Silent Lake is tailor-made for outdoors enthusiasts. Lakehead Loop is a leisurely stroll suitable for all ages (1.5 km) that is accessed right from the campground. Bonnie's Pond Trail is also an easy walk of 3 km that passes through forest, forest-fire burnt areas and a scenic lookout over Silent Lake. Lakeshore Hiking Trail is a more challenging (15 km) outing that encompasses swamps, beaver meadows and dense forest.

Silent Lake actually has three lakes. Silent Lake (named for the absence of motorboats) is connected to Quiet Lake and Soft Lake, and together these three supply excellent paddling around numerous islands. The park provides canoe and kayak rentals as well as canoe-in campsites.

Mountain-bike enthusiasts can also have their day in the sun at Silent Lake. The bike trail loops are 6, 12 and 19 km in length and are rated as moderately difficult to challenging. Muddy conditions are prevalent during spring.

Silent Lake is not only for backcountry experiences. The park has two beaches, the day-use beach being particularly good for fun, since it has a floating diving platform and a large picnic area and playing fields. While hunting is not permitted, fishing for trout and bass remains popular.

Silent Lake staff do a commendable job of highlighting the park's interesting features in a full interpretive program. The program includes talks, scavenger hunts, and lessons in canoeing, mountain biking, photography, fishing, geology and wildlife management. Special children's events and guided hikes are scheduled as well. The program runs in July and August.

Wintertime brings a striking, blue-and-white beauty to the park, and an outstanding experience awaits skiers. Forty kilometres of groomed, track-set trails await, crossing through silent forest and over those picturesque hills. Novices enjoy 2.5-km and 6-km trails. Slightly more advanced skiers tackle a 13-km trail, and experienced skiers love the demanding 19-km route. There is also an 8-km ski skating trail. Toilets and a warm-up shelter are provided, as is a simple camping area. Trails patrols are provided via the Canadian Ski Patrol Association. Other winter activities include snowshoeing and ice fishing.

Campground

Silent Lake's campsites are among the most picturesque in the province, located in a very hilly, wooded setting. The sites are well spaced out for privacy (even though many sites are without much undergrowth) and are quite large. Most sites have long driveways, which puts your tent or trailer farther from noise. Most of the campground roadways are paved to reduce dust problems. The park's 167 campsites (10 electrical) are located in two campgrounds, Granite Ridge and Pincer Bay.

Both campgrounds have steep, hilly sections unsuitable for large trailers—signs indicate which hills are too steep. Practically all sites in the park can be recommended, but the following are especially good campsites. Pincer Bay Campground: sites 7 and 62, with sites 1 and 2 recommended for two groups camping together. Granite Ridge campground: sites 110, 111, 134, 137, and 140; sites 125 and 126 for two groups travelling together.

Both campgrounds have excellent walk-in site areas, Pincer Bay's sites 66 to 73 being particularly close to a beach and sites 74 to 88 being closest to the canoe rental and dock area. Granite Ridge's walk-in sites 156 to 167 provide the best access to the day-use beach. The Lakeshore Hiking Trail runs through both campgrounds, while Pincer Bay has better access to the mountain-bike trail and Bonnie's Pond Trail. Both campgrounds have comfort stations with showers, toilets and laundry.

Silent Lake is unusual in offering two alternatives to conventional camping: a yurt and a 14-person lodge complete with kitchen, living areas and washrooms with showers, as well as bedrooms. Both the lodge and yurt are available for rentals year-round. The lodge is particularly ideal for family or business/social groups wanting quality time together in a natural setting.

Local Attractions

Bancroft (16 km) is the Mineral Capital of Canada—a treasure trove for amateurs and experts alike. The Old Station houses the Bancroft Mineral Museum with its extensive collection of specimens; the Art Gallery of Bancroft; and the North Hastings Heritage Museum. Bancroft hosts an annual August Gemboree when rock hounds from around the globe congregate to go collecting, buy and sell their wares, and attend talks and slide shows. All summer long, museum staff lead rock-hounding trips each Tuesday and Thursday. Have museum staff point the way to the spot in town where one can look for sodalite, a pretty blue mineral that is free for the taking. Ask for directions to the Dwyer Mine. For a small fee, you can hunt through the tailings from an abandoned mine.

For a completely different experience, travel to Petroglyphs Provincial Park (30 km) to see drawings of animals and figures etched on a sparkling white marble outcrop. These etchings are about 1,100 years old and are protected from the elements in a beautiful glass building. The park is located 40 minutes south of Silent Lake.

Fall brings spectacular colour to the forest—plum, scarlet, orange and bright yellow. A popular leaf-hunting drive is a loop starting and ending in Bancroft, passing through Maynooth and Combermere. Other good autumn drives include Apsley, Tory Hill and Gooderham.

The Mineral City Luge Club just east of Bancroft maintains an excellent luge facility, with both a snow track and an ice track. It's worth the climb to the mountain summit just for the eagle's-eye view of the surrounding hills that lay still under winter's white blanket. Equipment and lessons are provided at economical cost.

fast facts

Campgrounds: 167 sites in two campgrounds (10 sites with hydro hookups); 35 walk-in sites in campground; 40 interior sites. Group campsite. Yurts available; 14-person lodge available for rent during the winter. Comfort stations with showers and flush toilets (wheelchair accessible) and laundry. Camping season from mid-May to mid-October. Reservations recommended for all sites all season.

Supplies: Firewood and ice sold in the park. Groceries available near the park. Best shopping available in Bancroft (16 km).

Facilities:

Trailer sanitation station

Canoe and kayaking docking

Canoe and kayak rentals

Mountain-biking trails (6-, 12- and 19-km loops)

Hiking (three trails totalling 20 km)

Winter Use: The park has extensive cross-country trails (56 km). Winter accommodation in an unserviced campsite area or in the lodge (11-km ski to the lodge).

Contact Information: RR 2, Maberly ON, K0H 2B0 tel 613-268-2000

Restoule Provincial Park

Location: 45 km west of Highway 11 on Highway 534;
70 km south of North Bay.

Natural Environment: 2   **Activities: 1**   **Campground: 2**

Restoule Provincial Park may be less widely known than other parks in Ontario, but it is well worth an investigation, for it offers 1,100 hectares of mature mixed forest surrounding two pretty lakes. Attractive hiking trails lead to cliffs high over the shores of both Patterson (Stormy) and Restoule Lakes as well as to an old fire tower. Patterson Lake is popular for swimming, boating, mountain biking and fishing, and from the park canoeists can access the legendary French River routes used by voyageurs. Restoule's campsites are located on the lakeshore, and the group campground is one of the most attractive in the province.

Natural Environment and History

Restoule is a large park that occupies the land between two deep blue lakes just south of the scenic French River. The hills are covered with a variety of forest types that tell a story of both natural and human history. The tree cover is a mix of pine, spruce, maple and birch. In low-lying areas, damp and cold conditions encourage the growth of hemlock, while the thin soils of rocky hilltops support jack pine forest. The forest here is lovely in all seasons, with maple, birch and aspen turning vivid green in spring and a breathtaking range of hues in fall. In locations sheltered from the wind, snows stay on the boughs of pine and hemlock to create a Currier and Ives scene each winter.

The diversity of forest cover is reflected in the varied wildlife populations in the park. Hemlock swamps are particularly important as deer "yards," serving as a place of dependable forage and shelter for white-tailed deer. It is estimated that 10,000 deer spend their winter in the area just south of the park.

Although 19th-century settlers attempted, unsuccessfully, to farm the region that is now Restoule Park, it was later foresters who made a permanent living here off the riches of huge trees. The descendants of both farmers and loggers now share the land's bounty with tourist operators and many artisans.

Special Activities

Restoule offers a variety of ways to enjoy the outdoors. Hikers tackle two self-guiding nature trails. The River Trail (2 km) traces the footpaths that may have been used by explorer Champlain or later fur-traders. The Tower Trail (7 km) is much recommended for the extraordinary vista 60 m above pristine Patterson Lake. This overlook (near an old fire tower) is one of the best places to enjoy real serenity in Southern Ontario.

The park is also ideal for enjoying water-based fun. Three beaches have a total of 600 m of sandy, shallow swimming; the main beach has a volleyball area and a playground. Boats may be launched on both Patterson and Stormy Lakes. The Patterson launch area includes dockage. Windsurfing and water skiing are both enjoyed in the park.

Fishing is good in the park and connecting waterways. Although pike, bass and lake trout are caught here, the pickerel is the centre of attention, and the local community is active in habitat improvement for this sweetest of game fish. You don't need a boat to fish Restoule. Just where the river passes through a section of rapids, there is a cedar-shaded fishing and picnic spot complete with benches and picnic tables. It's hard to imagine a more picturesque place to while away a summer afternoon. It is canoeists who may love the park the best, for it is an excellent base for an exploration of the French River, one of the province's most important 19th-century trade routes, and known now for good fishing and fabulous scenery.

Cyclists also have their day in the sun at Restoule. Three biking trails total 10 km in length. Ranger's Point Trail is an easy ride for families; Angel's Point has two trails, each about 2 km in length, that are suitable for novices. The Gibs Trail is currently under development, but cyclists are permitted to explore the unmarked and unmaintained trail. The park rents bicycles.

Park staff coordinate a program of activities with events taking place several times weekly. Survival games, baseball games, illustrated talks, scavenger hunts and guided hikes are typical program elements.

Campground

Restoule Provincial Park has three campgrounds with a total of 278 campsites (97 electrical). Because much of the forest in the campground is young, there is plenty of undergrowth to provide privacy between sites. Sites in the central portion of the campgrounds can be rather hemmed in by other campers, so preferred sites are on the water or closest to the park interior.

The best sites are numbers 424 to 432 (even numbers) and 440 in Kettle Point Campground; these are electrical sites. Although some sites within Putts Point Campground are close to a beach, the sites here are more densely spaced. The Bell's Point Campground are among the most private in the park, especially numbers 30 to 36 (even numbers) and 37 to 43 (odd numbers). Sites 151 to 160 are walk-in sites on a small peninsula. Although these sites are private, several of them are rather close to a damp area and may be buggy. However, some of these sites (for instance, numbers 155 to 157) have lovely water views.

Local Attractions

Although Central Ontario was at one time strictly a region for sportsmen, that has greatly altered, so many interesting daytrips that can be made from Restoule Provincial Park. The park can provide a detailed guide to art studios and antique shops hidden in the surrounding countryside. Nipissing, Callander, Powassan and Commanda all have local history museums. Commanda's museum is in a historic general store that doubles as a tea room with light meals and baked goods. Further afield is North Bay, the point of departure for the *Chief Commanda II*. Passengers enjoy four- and five-hour cruises from North Bay to the entrance to the French River. Shorter cruises concentrate on the shoreline and islands of Lake Nipissing. Friday-evening cruises may include dancing or other entertainment.

fast facts

Campgrounds: 278 sites in three campgrounds (97 sites with hydro hookups); some sites wheelchair accessible. Group camping. Seasonal leasing. Comfort stations with showers and flush toilets (wheelchair accessible). Camping season from late May to mid-October. Reservations recommended for all sites in July and August.

Supplies: Firewood and ice sold in park. Modest supplies available near the park from general stores. Better shopping available in Powassan or Trout Creek (each about 45 km).

Facilities:
Trailer sanitation station
Trailer and boat storage
Boat launches and docking
Beach
Sports fields
Bike rentals
Mountain bike trails (three trails totalling 10 km)
Hiking trails (two trails totalling 9 km)

Winter Use: The park is closed in winter.

Contact Information: Restoule ON, P0H 2R0 tel 705-729-2010

Killarney Provincial Park

Location: 250 km north of Parry Sound and 100 km south of
   Sudbury. About 60 km west of Highway 69 on Highway 637.
Natural Environment: 3   Activities: 2   Campground: 1

A visit to Killarney Provincial Park is like stepping into a Group of Seven painting—all wind-twisted pine, craggy shoreline and bare hills that undulate to the horizon. The La Cloche Mountains of Killarney are indeed the favourite subject of scores of artists and it seems that in every direction lies a panorama worthy of a painting. Dozens of lakes are encircled by sparkling white quartzite or by iron-red granite dramatically streaked with volcanic black. Killarney's 48,500 hectares have some of Ontario's best backcountry hiking and canoe routes, as well as many adventures closer to the campground. The Georgian Bay village of Killarney is a short drive from the park, and beckons to daytrippers with sailing, sea kayaking, historic sites and a small commercial fishery.

Natural Environment and History

It seems as if so many superlatives have been used to convey Killarney's beauty that there are few words left to use. What's interesting is that this natural grandeur is in large part due to geologic events that occurred eons ago. Rock-forming processes of intense heat and pressure created huge jagged mountains of remarkable colouration. Although glaciation and erosion whittled the mountains into rounded hills, the remarkable colouration of the rock remains the dominant feature of the landscape. Northern Killarney is characterized by the La Cloche Mountains of pure, sparkling white quartzite. The area of the park south of George Lake is characterized by strikingly red granite.

Killarney's forests are also determined by this geologic diversity. Pockets of fertile soil deposited by glaciers in valley bottoms support healthy forests of maple, birch, aspen, ash and oak. On the ridges, barren and arid conditions prevail and limit plant growth to a variety of colourful lichens, mosses and stunted pine. These bands of forest alternate up the hillsides, and when autumn brings its annual foliage display, the colour contrast is breathtaking.

Animals, too, have adapted to the varying environments in the park. At lower levels, moose, beaver, deer and small mammals are common. Ravens, turkey vultures, and hawks soar on the thermals over the cliffs. Killarney has been especially hard hit by acid rain, so fish life in the park is poor. Although the lakes are recovering, thanks to recent pollution control measures, these waters are still considered fish sanctuaries.

The human history of Killarney is also remarkably diverse. Archaeological evidence indicates that hunting camps were established here as long ago as 9,000 years. Much more recently, hunters, loggers, fishermen and farmers all worked in the region. The appeal of the scenery to the arts community is a development of the 20th century. One of the park's lakes—O.S.A. Lake—was named after the Ontario Society of Artists because of their role in ensuring Killarney received provincial park status.

Special Activities

Killarney has some of the best hiking trails and canoe routes in Ontario—and that is a considerable claim. Three short trails are in close proximity to the campground. The trail guides available at the visitor centre are among the best produced in the province and add value to any hike. The Cranberry Bog Trail (4 km) passes by three distinct wetland types: marshes, bogs and swamps. Chikanishing Trail works your legs on many ascents and descents along a rocky 3-km route to Georgian Bay. The Granite Ridge Trail (2 km) is the best trail to hike if you have only a short stay in the park. It ascends rather steeply to a magnificent 270-degree vista that takes in Georgian Bay, offshore islands, and the La Cloche Mountains. Energetic and prepared hikers test their fitness on the 100-km-long La Cloche Silhouette Trail. This trail is for experienced hikers only.

Canoeists often choose Killarney as their favourite base camp for trips. This is because so many of the park's lakes are long and narrow, so that it is possible to canoe for long distances without portaging. Canoeing on Georgian Bay is challenging and often dangerous; our "sixth Great Lake" is best left to sailors and experienced sea-kayakers.

Outfitters located near the park rent paddling and hiking equipment and maps. Canoe racks near the main campground beach are well stocked by several companies, and once payment is made for a canoe (in person or by phone), renters receive a lock combination so they can access the canoes. This service makes outbound adventures all the easier.

During the winter, adventurers make use of unserviced camping and backcountry skiing and snowshoeing. The ski trails are not groomed and are 8, 12 and 14 km in length.

Park staff present guided hikes and talks. The programming is rich in educational value. Topics presented may include backpacking equipment, canoe instruction, park insects, birdwatching, creatures of the night, stargazing and edible wild plants.

Campground

The George Lake Campground has 122 campsites. Because Killarney is a wilderness class park, the facilities are fairly simple: two beaches, vault toilets (some barrier-free), water taps—and not much else. The campsites at Killarney are, at first glance, rather disappointing, with high density and low privacy. But with careful planning and reservations, you can secure a reasonable degree of privacy. The best sites are in the Trout Creek area (sites 11 through 30); these have better privacy than other parts of the campground. Other good sites include the following: 48, 63, 70, 71 to 74 (four sites good for a group), 80 and 81 (good for two families), 84, 108, 111, 137 and 138. Hikers and canoeists make use of 168 interior campsites.

The Friends of Killarney operate a truly excellent store in the main park office. In addition to trail guides (and expert advice on hiking or canoeing plans), the store sells books, artwork, and camping accessories.

Local Attractions

The village of Killarney is only 12 km from the park entrance, and is worthy of at least a half-day's visit for its historic sites and small history museum. Every visitor should partake of the freshly caught whitefish or trout at the fish-and-chippery located near the town dock and enjoy the meal on the sundeck. The 7-km Tar Vat Trail begins at the town's East Lighthouse and leads to Pond Point, a small bay where fishermen once tarred their nets.

Fast Facts

Campgrounds: 122 sites; some campsites are wheelchair accessible; 112 backcountry sites. Comfort stations with showers and toilets (accessible). Campground open all year. Reservations recommended for all sites, all summer long.

Supplies: Firewood and ice are sold in the park. Basic supplies available in Killarney (12 km) and at local outfitters. Complete shopping is far away, so plan on stocking up before reaching the park.

Facilities:
- Trailer sanitation station
- Canoe rentals arranged through local outfitters
- Boat launch to Georgian Bay (no motors in park)
- Beaches
- Hiking (three trails total 9 km; overnight hiking totalling 100 km)

Winter Use: The park is open in winter for cross-country skiing (34 km of ungroomed trails) and unserviced camping.

Contact Information: Killarney ON, P0M 2A0 tel 705-287-2900

Killbear Provincial Park

Location: About 35 km northwest of Parry Sound;
20 km west of Highway 69 along Highway 559.
Natural Environment: 2   **Activities: 2**   **Campground: 2**

Killbear Provincial Park is one of the most spectacularly beautiful places in Ontario, and certainly the best location for letting Georgian Bay's blustery wildness fill your senses. Rocky headlands shelter fine white sand beaches; trails lead to lookouts high over picturesque Parry Sound; verdant woodlands are habitat for abundant wildlife. Killbear is one of Ontario's most popular parks, and many families consider this spot their personal summer home. Despite heavy use all summer long, the campgrounds are quite satisfactory. Excellent park programs and top-notch local attractions make for an active summer holiday.

Natural Environment and History

Killbear has a long, long history; in fact, some geologists speculate that the exposed bedrock on the hills and along the shore may be the oldest rock on Earth. Perhaps this is the reason that a shoreline hike at sunset has a timeless feel to it. Wind, waves and several ice ages have had their way with that twisted rock, so that what once were ragged mountains are now round hills, and instead of craggy outcrops, the granite undulates and folds—rather like landscape-sized sculptures.

The park sits astride the boundary between northern and southern landscapes, its northern climate moderated by the influence of the Great

Lakes. Most of the park is thickly forested with maple, oak, birch, pine and spruce, the species varying with elevation.

The best-known resident of the park is the endangered Massasauga rattlesnake, and Killbear has one of the largest remaining populations of this fascinating (but shy) species. Park naturalists conduct leading-edge research, and many of the park's snakes are outfitted with radio transmitters. Other park residents include include fox snake, spotted turtle, fox, deer and bear.

Special Activities

With such a splendid natural setting, it's no wonder that nature appreciation is at the heart of all outings at Killbear. All three of the park's hiking trails are very good. The Lighthouse Lookout Trail leads to Killbear Point, a good spot for recording Georgian Bay sunsets on film. Lookout Point Trail (3.5 km) is a trip through several types of forest and leads to Blind Bay. The Twin Points Trail (2 km) explores the rocky shore and woods near the day-use beach. The ancient, weathered shoreline rock here forms tiny nooks smooth enough for excellent sunbathing out of the Bay's chill winds. Long-distance exploration will become even easier in the future, when a park-to-park trail connecting Killlbear, Algonquin, Oastler Lake and Arrowhead Provincial Parks is completed.

Canoeists and kayakers spend countless hours exploring the 30,000 Islands, many of which have picnic spots. Parry Sound is renowned for sailing and motor cruising, and these are also enjoyed at Killbear. The park has several boat launches and a boat basin for shallow-water anchorage. Fisherfolk ply the deep waters for bass, lake trout, whitefish, pickerel and pike. Despite the chill in Georgian Bay's waters that lingers until midsummer, the park's several beaches and the rocky headlands are well used by swimmers.

Don't visit the park without taking a cruise aboard the M.V. *Chippewa*. This cruise ship departs from the Lighthouse Point Campground for two-hour excursions through the 30,000 Islands. You can even partake of more than one cruise, since a variety of routes are followed.

Killbear has two centres for nature education. The main visitor centre near the park entrance has art displays with a focus on wildlife and nature. The tiny interpretive centre is the place to find out about the active program of educational events. Guided hikes take place weekly; evening movies, slide shows and campfires take place at least twice a week. Spirit walks and musical entertainment are scheduled during the busy summer months. Daily children's events include arts and crafts, games or short outings. The interpretive centre also has displays on the wildlife and plants found in the park.

When snow blankets drooping evergreen boughs and a hush falls over the land, visitors find that they have this huge park all to themselves. Intrepid skiers head out on 30 km of groomed trails; snowshoers can bushwack through the backwoods. Killbear rents their staff house (with or without catering); the building can accommodate up to 30 people.

Campground

Killbear's campground is huge—over 800 campsites in seven camp-grounds. The park does a good job of identifying the best campsites by charging a premium fee for waterside locations. This is a heavily used park, and many sites are not particularly private. However, the camper in the know reserves a good site ahead of time. All campgrounds except for Granite Saddle have comfort stations with showers and flush toilets. The following campgrounds have laundries: Beaver Dams, Kilcoursie Bay and Harold Point.

If proximity to a beach is important, then head for the following campgrounds (best sites noted in brackets): Kilcoursie Bay (53 to 57, 66 and 68); Beaver Dams (288, 316, 317 and 326); Harold Point (528, 620 and 631); Lighthouse Point (1106 and 1108); or Granite Saddle (1038 and 1039). Radio-free zones are available in Granite Saddle, Harold Point and Lighthouse Point (sites 1400 to 1497).

The sites in Granite Saddle have the advantage of lower traffic levels. The sites in Kilcoursie Bay, Harold Point and Beaver Dams overlook the busy boat anchoring harbour. Although the big cruisers and sailboats are picturesque, the noise level from boats and from jet skis really detracts from the camping experience. The quietest campground is Blind Bay, which has one side of the Killbear peninsula all to itself. Boaters prefer the sites in Blind Bay close to the water in order to beach their craft at their campsite.

Local Attractions

The natural beauty of the 30,000 Islands (the largest concentration of islands in the world) attracts sightseers from around the world. The *Island Queen*, a triple-decked cruise boat, departs from Parry Sound several times daily during the summer. Appreciating the islands from the air is also popular, and seaplanes depart from near the *Island Queen* docks for fly-in fishing flights and sightseeing flights.

One of Ontario's best annual events is Parry Sound's Festival of the Sound, which offers over four dozen musical events over three weeks each midsummer. The events are in a variety of venues, from concerts in local parks, to dinner and music cruises, or events hosted in private homes.

High on a hill overlooking Parry Sound is the West Parry Sound District Museum. Displays depict local history, including the exciting era of logging and shipping. The gardens and lookout at the museum are a wonderful picnic site.

Fast Facts

Campgrounds: 882 campsites in seven campgrounds (147 sites with hydro hookups); some wheelchair-accessible campsites. Comfort stations with flush toilets, showers and laundry (some laundries may not be wheelchair accessible). Camping season mid-May to mid-October. Reservations recommended for all sites all summer.

Supplies: Firewood sold in the park. The park store has basic groceries, as do stores near the park entrance, but the best shopping is in Parry Sound (about 40 km).

Facilities:
Trailer sanitation station
Boat launch and boat anchoring area, but no docking
Beaches
Boat cruises
Interpretive centre
Hiking trails (three trails totalling about 6.5 km)

Winter Use: The park is closed in winter.

Contact Information: Box 71, Nobel ON, P0G 1G0 tel 705-342-5492

Grundy Lake Provincial Park

Location: 80 km north of Parry Sound just off Highway 69.

Natural Environment: 2   **Activities:** 3   **Campground:** 1

Grundy Lake is one of Ontario's most popular family holiday parks. Hundreds of campsites are located on four different lakes, and each campground has its own appeal. One might have a beach with a diving platform, while another is close to the volleyball court and visitor centre. The purpose of the park's visitor program is to make the lakes accessible to one and all. Campers enjoy paddleboat, kayak and canoe rentals; hiking trails (including boardwalks over lakes); beaches on four lakes; and a continually active program of nature-centred activities. Wildlife viewing opportunities abound here and the park is especially well known for its beaver lodges and active heronry.

Natural Environment and History

Although Grundy Lake protects over 2,500 hectares of waterways and forest, it is not a park of large scenic vistas as much as a place to enjoy nature's delights close at hand. Here you'll discover the perfect picnic spot tucked into sun-warmed rocks; a loon family taking a moonlit swim; a beaver floating an aspen branch to its lodge.

One of Grundy Lake's special features is the large number of wetlands where shallow water permits the growth of aquatic vegetation. Botanists visit these areas for the abundance and variety of flowers. The wetlands are also premium wildlife-viewing locations, and racoon, fox and beaver are commonly seen, as are loons and ducks. For decades Grundy Lake has been a popular place to visit a large and noisy heronry where great blue herons construct their bulky stick-nests high in dead trees in a swamp. The heronry is easily observed from one of the park trails.

Any camper can tell you that the berry picking is especially good at Grundy Lake, and strawberries, raspberries and blueberries are common throughout the campground.

Special Activities

Park staff make it easy for anyone to be active outdoors. Canoe launches and rentals of canoes, kayaks and paddleboats relieve the hassle of getting organized for exploring the park's many lakes. A local outfitter will even deliver canoes to your campsite and pick them up at specified times. Even on the busiest lakes—Grundy, Gurd and Gut—there are plenty of quiet inlets to paddle, rocky headlands and beaches for swimming and islands perfect for shore lunches. Take a rod and reel with you, because Grundy has healthy populations of pickerel, pike, bass, bullhead and panfish. Motorboats are not permitted in the park.

Hiking is also popular in the park, and three trails are easy walks for those of any age. (A fourth longer and more demanding trail is under construction.) Swan Lake Trail is a 1.5-km loop around a small lake. Extensive boardwalk sections allow an up-close look at bog and marshes where painted turtles sun on floating logs, bitterns stalk frogs and osprey wheel overhead. Plants seen en route include leatherleaf, cranberry, and bog laurel. The 4-km Beaver Dam Trail is the best place to see the dam-builders at work as well as the heronry. Gut Lake Trail (2.5 km) scrambles over pink granite outcrops and past wetlands—a scenic outing for photographers.

Park naturalists run a wide variety of programs, and events take place throughout the park—usually several times daily. The program has the typical elements: evening presentations of skits, shows, films and special guests; guided hikes by foot and canoe; junior naturalist events for children; and recreation events such as volleyball games and canoe and kayak demonstrations.

Campground

Grundy Lake has a huge area devoted to campers: nine campgrounds on four lakes, each with a comfort station, and most with their own beach. Of the park's 460 campsites, 80 have electrical hookups. A brief description of each campground follows.

Poplar, Trailer and Hemlock campgrounds are on pretty Gurd Lake. Poplar and Trailer Campgrounds have electrical sites, and many are pull-throughs for trailers. The beach shared by Trailer and Hemlock is one of the best in the park, uncrowded, and with a deluxe platform and diving board. The nicest sites in these three areas are Poplar sites 303 to 305 and 315 and Hemlock sites 112 and 115 to 122.

White Spruce is the smallest campground and therefore one of the quietest. The best sites are number 21 and 22, which overlook Gut Lake. White Spruce is closest to a trail that leads to Gurd Lake Dam and is also convenient to the interpretive centre, amphitheatre and beach volleyball court. Red Maple and White Pine are both large, densely packed and rather busy campgrounds on Grundy Lake. Red Maple is a radio-free zone and has a good beach with floating platform. The best site in these areas is number 500 in White Pine. White Pine has the best access to the main park beach and is also close to the amphitheatre and interpretive centre.

Two smaller campgrounds are White Birch and Jack Pine; both campgrounds are on Grundy Lake. White Birch has a small beach area. Site 654 is recommended, and the following have nice views of the lake: sites 643 to 645 and 638. White Birch sites are a little larger than those in the rest of the park. Good though rather open sites in Jack Pine are numbers 732 and 733. The most remote campground is Balsam. Although the sites here are large and lovely, especially numbers 826, 829 and 837, busy Highway 69 is just across small Clear Lake, and highway noise is a definite detraction. This campground has no beach.

Local Attractions

Grundy Lake Provincial Park is not easily accessible to important tourist attractions. Sudbury is an hour's drive to the north, but is well worth a day for the Big Nickel Mine Tour and Science North, with its IMAX theatre, daily demonstrations and virtual adventure rides. (See Halfway Lake Provincial Park.) Parry Sound, almost as far to the south of Grundy Lake as Sudbury is to the north, offers *Island Queen* boat cruises, a good local history museum and midsummer's fabulous Festival of the Sound, a three-week extravaganza of music. (See Killbear Provincial Park.)

Fast Facts

Campgrounds: 460 sites in nine campgrounds (80 sites with hydro hookups); some sites wheelchair accessible; 10 backcountry sites. Group campgrounds. Seasonal leasing. Comfort stations with showers, flush toilets and laundry (accessible). Camping season mid-May to mid-October. Reservations recommended for hydro sites and waterfront sites on long weekends.

Supplies: Firewood is sold in the park. Some groceries and an ice-cream stand are one kilometre away. Better grocery shopping is in Parry Sound (80 km).

Facilities:

Trailer sanitation stations

Trailer storage

Boat launch but no dockage

Canoe, kayak and paddleboat rentals

Visitor centre (accessible)

Beaches

Horseshoe pits

Sports fields including volleyball and softball fields

Hiking trails (three trails totalling 8.5 km)

Winter Use: The park is gated in winter.

Contact Information: RR 1, Britt ON, P0G 1A0 tel 705-383-2369

Awenda Provincial Park

Location: 11 km north of Penetanguishene off Highway 93.
Natural Environment: 2   Activities: 3   Campground: 3

Georgian Bay's breathtaking scenery of a wide blue horizon dotted with rocky islands awaits discovery at Awenda Provincial Park. Awenda's 2,000 ha protect the last remaining undeveloped shoreline on southern Georgian Bay. Although most park campers visit to enjoy the scenic shoreline, Awenda is also remarkable for its inland topography, a jumble of bluffs, ridges and lakes created by glaciers thousands of years ago. Awenda was home to early aboriginals, and the artifacts of four different cultures make the park an archaeological treasure trove. The park's four beaches are unusual in that glacial boulders are scattered along the pure white sands and shallow water, so that it's possible to combine rock scrambling and swimming. Hiking, canoeing, fishing and cross-country skiing are also popular activities at Awenda.

Natural Environment and History

Awenda's verdant forest is the first physical feature you encounter upon entering the park. Unlike most parks in Central Ontario, the forest at Awenda is predominantly deciduous. Loggers removed the original oak and pine a century ago, but the second-growth maple, oak and ash are already sufficiently large and lofty to spread ample shade. The undergrowth is particularly dense, and even in droughty summers provides a lush green backdrop for campsites.

The topography in the park is a ready-made lesson on glaciation; it's as if the giant ice sheets decided to put all their works in one special display. Beaches of boulders and cobble, sand dune ridges (now heavily forested) and a round kettle lake (called Kettle's Lake) are all the work of ages past. Nipissing Bluff is the most significant piece of topography, and hikers can climb up and down this 60-m promontory on several trails.

The most enjoyed pieces of Awenda's natural beauty are the wide beaches along Georgian Bay. The Bay is never warm, but its chill is lessened in these shallow, sandy coves. Just offshore, Giant's Tomb Island is also part of Awenda Provincial Park. Boaters visit the island for picnicking, camping and swimming.

Special Activities

Watersports are a highlight of a visit to Awenda. The park's four sheltered beaches are not only ideal for family swimming, but they have scenic views of Georgian Bay's distant islands. The glaciers were at work here, too, leaving behind a jumble of boulders small and huge on the sands, and these make good play features for beachcombers, look-out perches for shorebirds, and refuges for small water critters. The best beach of all is at Methodist Point.

Boating is popular at Awenda, though there is no boat launch. Pike, bass and pickerel are caught in Georgian Bay, and bass fishing is popular in tiny, uncrowded Kettle's Lake. Canoeists also head for Kettle's Lake to avoid the unpredictable winds and waves of Georgian Bay.

Awenda's many hiking trails provide excellent exercise in lovely scenery, and many are easy enough for family outings. Seven trails total 30 km of enjoyment. Beaver Pond Trail is barrier-free, and includes a boardwalk, a platform lookout over a beaver pond, as well as picnic facilities. The Bluff Trail is the longest route, at 13 km, and is thus a favourite of cyclists, who use the trail to access terrific views of Georgian Bay from the Nipissing Bluff. The park has an all-terrain wheelchair available for public use.

Staff run an interpretive program that includes children's activities, guided hikes, corn roasts, photography tours and evening programs. Many of these events are held in the activity centre.

Awenda is a busy park during the "off season." Cross-country skiing takes place on 30 km of track-set and marked trails for all skill levels, and off-trail snowshoeing is popular as well. A trail centre is open during winter, with shelter and a wood stove for warming up.

Campground

Awenda's 325 campsites are located in six campgrounds, each named for a different Huron clan. Each site is sheltered under huge maples and oak and is within an easy walk of a comfort station, and each campground has at least one wheelchair accessible site. As with most parks created in recent decades, the campgrounds are designed for maximum campsite privacy and reduced traffic. Three campgrounds, Deer, Bear and Snake, are designated radio-free. Although all sites in the park are excellent, Snake Campground has perhaps the nicest sites of all, with long driveways and very wide spaces between sites. The hydro sites (Wolf Campground) are more densely spaced than the sites in the other campgrounds.

Local Attractions

Awenda is well located to take advantage of the many attractions of Pene-tanguishene and Midland. Discovery Harbour in Penetanguishene is one of Ontario's premier historic attractions. This reconstructed British naval depot was a busy place in the early 1800s, and its bustling shipyard and village are busy once again. Sign up for a cruise aboard two replica schooners carefully modelled after 1812 British naval ships or enjoy a horse-drawn ride through the village of barracks, doctor's office, cartographer's house and commander's house. The walking tours with costumed staff are highly recommended. Restaurant and shops are on-site.

Midland has its own historic sites worth visiting. Ste. Marie Among the Hurons is an accurate reconstruction of a 17th-century Jesuit mission, one of Ontario's first European settlements. After viewing a film that puts the settlement into its fascinating historical context, visitors step into a living village of costumed staff who play the roles of missionaries, Christian Huron converts and other settlers. Crafts, drama presentations and canoe cruises are part of an active interpretive program. Iroquois killed several of the Jesuits at Ste. Marie, and six of those killed were canonized. Their memory is preserved at Martyrs' Shrine, a massive white church sits high on the hill just across the highway from Ste. Marie. Pilgrims come from around the world to attend mass here.

Midland's Huronia Museum also celebrates the past, with a large collection of artifacts and documents that record local history from the time of the Huron to the mid-20th century. The museum includes a recreated Huron village complete with cedar palisades, longhouses, cooking fires, a medicine man's lodge and lookout tower. The museum gallery displays works by artists such as A. Y. Jackson and Frank Johnston as well as by local painters.

fast facts

Campgrounds: 325 sites in six campgrounds (72 with hydro hookups); some sites wheelchair accessible. Group camping. Comfort stations with flush toilets and showers (accessible) and laundries. Camping season from mid-May to mid-October. Reservations recommended during midsummer for all sites.

Supplies: Ice and firewood sold in the park. Shopping available in Penetanguishene (20 km) and Midland (25 km).

Facilities:
Trailer sanitation station
Beaches
Activity centre
Hiking trails (seven trails totalling 30 km; one trail barrier-free)

Winter Use: The park has 28 km of cross-country ski trails with warm-up hut.

Contact Information: Box 5904, Penetanguishene ON, L9M 2G2 tel 705-549-2231

SOUTHWESTERN ONTARIO

Bruce Peninsula National Park

Location: 7 km south of Tobermory, off Highway 6,
    near the tip of the Bruce Peninsula.
Natural Environment: 3   Activities: 3   Campground: 3

The Bruce Peninsula can easily rival any beauty spot on the globe for the photogenic arrangement of towering cliffs, dazzling turquoise waters, foam-speckled coves and dozens of unusual plants and animals. The park's 140 square kilometres have a natural attraction to suit every interest. Botanists hunt for rare ferns, orchids and ancient cedars; biologists study uncommon bat species; and geologists hunt for fossils. Adventurers explore underwater caves and shipwrecks, kayak into charming coves, and tramp the long-distance Bruce Trail. Holiday-makers enjoy beaches, boating, fishing, and ply the waters off Tobermory in glass-bottom boats. Bruce Peninsula National Park also provides a warm-water beach on an interior lake, cycling, and a good campground.

Natural Environment and History

The dominating feature of the park is Ontario's ancient, rocky backbone, the Niagara Escarpment, which forms the 40-m-tall cliff face on Georgian Bay. Four hundred million years ago, when eastern North America lay under a warm sea, the skeletal remains of countless small sea creatures combined with ocean sediments to form a high promontory of hard dolomite bedrock. The Escarpment is a familiar landmark to Ontarians, since it extends through Southern Ontario, from the tip of the Bruce Peninsula through to Niagara (and beyond), and is one of the province's best-known landmarks.

The Escarpment, although rocky, seems perfect for growing things. Loggers harvested the region's original forest, so the current forest of cedar, fir and aspen is second-growth. However, those stunted cliff-hugging cedars seen along the trails are the oldest trees in Ontario (estimated to be 1,600 years old), spared from the logger's axe due to their inaccessibility. Other rare or uncommon plants in the park include 20 species of

GEORGIAN BAY

LAKE HURON

OWEN SOUND

BARRIE

LAKE SIMCOE

LAKE ONTARIO

TORONTO

HAMILTON

NIAGARA FALLS

QEW

LONDON

WINDSOR

LAKE ERIE

38
6
39
40
21
41
40
42
43
45
7
44
401
26
6
7
11
69
11
35
60
7
400

SOUTHWESTERN ONTARIO

LEGEND

38 Bruce Peninsula National Park
39 MacGregor Point Provincial Park
40 Falls Reserve Conservation Area
41 Pinery Provincial Park
42 Rondeau Provincial Park
43 Wheatley Provincial Park
44 Port Burwell Provincial Park
45 Elora Gorge Conservation Area

fern, 43 orchids and five insect-eating plants. Not only do multi-coloured lichens and mosses live on the rocks themselves, but this location is one of the few places on Earth where plant life exists within rocks—called cryptoendolithic life.

The rocks of the Escarpment form nooks and crannies custom-made for nesting turkey vultures, swallows, bats and ravens. The endangered Massasauga rattlesnake, Ontario's only venomous snake, also inhabits the park, though it is rarely seen. You will not likely see bears and coyotes on the trails, but deer, racoon and porcupine are frequently encountered. Birdwatchers visit the park throughout the seasons, but especially during fall migration, when thousands of hawks migrate along the Escarpment.

Special Activities

Any visit to the Bruce Peninsula means that it's time to don hiking boots. The four major trails in the park are accessed at the Head of Trails, where visitors may check their bearing on the trail map and refresh at the water tap. The most recommended excursion is the 3-km Georgian Bay–Marr Lake Trail that connects the Head of Trails to the waterside route of the legendary Bruce Trail. Upon reaching the cliffs, hikers may travel north or south—either direction is spectacularly beautiful. Highlights of the Georgian Bay–Marr Lake Trail are the caves at Indian Head Cove; named the Grotto and the Natural Arch, they a favourite haunt of scuba divers. The cove is always photogenic, but no more so than when half a dozen brightly coloured sea kayaks rest on the white pebble beach. Views from Overhanging Rock include distant Bears Rump Island and Flowerpot Island. Although the boulder beach en route to Marr Lake can be a tiresome scramble, it is a short distance from the boulders to the more easily travelled return leg of the trail.

Horse Lake Trail is a short, one-kilometre walk from Head of Trails to Georgian Bay. A circular loop around interior Cyprus Lake is best for young families because of its relatively level, easy conditions and shorter length (0.5 km). The trail also provides access from the campground to the Head of Trails.

For adventurous types, the Bruce Trail travels 736 km from Tobermory to Niagara. Eighteen campsites located along the trail must be reserved ahead of your hike. Because the Bruce Peninsula is prime territory for outdoor enthusiasts, outfitters in nearby Tobermory can provide equipment and other necessities for sea kayaking, scuba diving and other activities.

Hiking and kayaking are not the only activities in the park. Swimming takes place at two small beaches on interior Cyprus Lake. The roads in the park are very good for cycling. Cycling is not permitted on park trails.

Park staff run a program of special events such as movie nights, special lecturers, guided hikes both day and night within the park and to local natural areas such as Flowerpot Island. The Friends of Bruce Peninsula National Park organize several special events in the park, such as pancake breakfasts and a junior lightkeeper's program.

Campground

Bruce Peninsula National Park provides 233 campsites in three campgrounds on Cyprus Lake. National park campgrounds, and this one is no exception, are well-planned and feature spacious sites and good privacy. The campground lacks a comfort station, and has only vault toilets. The Tamarack Campground is the best of the lot for privacy, and the following sites are especially recommended: sites 202, 204, 207, 208, 211, 212, 215, 239, 252, 257, 258, 264 and 265. Tamarack is for tenters only. The Birches Campground is mainly pull-through sites for trailers. The Poplars Campground has some nice sites, such as number 15, 17, 45, 55 and 43. Poplars is closest to the Head of Trails.

Local Attractions

Tobermory is a delightful destination for daytrips or for full vacations. It has a pretty location on a sheltered harbour where fishing boats and pleasure craft rock in the waves. Brightly coloured buildings house art galleries, souvenir shops and several restaurants serving fresh local whitefish.

Tobermory is the point of departure for trips to Flowerpot Island, so named for the tall, narrow "sea stacks" of eroded rock along the shoreline that resemble flowerpots. The island is famous for orchids, gigantic toads, birdwatching and great hiking. Reservable campsites on the island administered by Bruce Peninsular National Park. Glass-bottom boat tours are popular outings from Tobermory as well. Cruisers get close-up looks at two 20th-century shipwrecks.

More than 22 shipwrecks await scuba divers in Fathom Five National Park. Extremely clear water, underwater caves and the wrecks combine to make Tobermory a hotbed of diving. The 20 islands of Fathom Five are beloved by sea kayakers. Fishing, diving and kayaking outings can be arranged in Tobermory.

The Bruce Peninsula has many natural attractions outside the park proper. Singing Sands is a warm, very shallow beach on the Lake Huron side of the peninsula named for the eerie sound the wind makes as it passes over the sand. A boardwalk leads through wetlands. The Dorcas Bay Nature Preserve is the property of the Federation of Ontario Naturalists, but is open to the public. At both of these fragile preserves you'll see wildflower photographers busy with giant lenses and reflective foil, trying for the perfect shot of beauties such as fragrant white bog orchid or yellow lady's-slipper. Best blooms are usually mid-June to early July.

The Bruce Peninsula offers some great pleasure drives as well. Villages worth visiting include Dyer's Bay and Lion's Head. Local tourist offices can supply information on lighthouses, caves, art studios and other points of interest.

Fast Facts

Campgrounds: 233 campsites in three campgrounds; 18 backcountry
   sites. Group campgrounds. No comfort stations, no sites with
   hydro hookups. Camping season mid-May to mid-October.
   Reservations recommended mid-May to early September.

Supplies: Firewood sold in park. Supplies available in Tobermory
   (10 km).

Facilities:
   Trailer sanitation area
   Beaches
   Hiking trails (four trails totalling 4.5 km, plus access to the
      Bruce Trail)

Winter Use: The park is gated in the winter.

Contact Information: Box 189, Tobermory ON, N0H 2R0
   tel 519-596-2233

MacGregor Point Provincial Park

Location: About 10 km south of Port Elgin, between
   Lake Huron and Highway 21.
Natural Environment: 1   Activities: 3   Campground: 3

Some of Ontario's most precious natural resources are the small remnants of natural Great Lakes shoreline, especially along highly developed Lakes Erie and Huron coast. MacGregor Point Provincial Park protects a long, beautiful stretch of windswept beaches and inland wetlands with opportunities for hiking, cycling, boating and fishing that in itself would make the basis of a great park. MacGregor Point is one of Ontario's newest parks, established when Inverhuron Park was closed for camping because of the construction of the Bruce Nuclear Power Plant. Planners relied on decades of experience in campground design, park layout and visitor programming to create a truly superb camping and outdoors experience.

Natural Environment and History

Twelve thousand years ago, receding glaciers left behind them a complex jumble of landforms along Lake Huron's shore. Each landform—such as the shoreline of prehistoric Lake Algonquin—created a microhabitat where a unique assemblage of plants and animals thrive. This outstanding diversity and MacGregor Point's extensive size (1,200 ha) mean that it's possible to visit several distinct communities within a day: treed swamps, upland forest, cattail marshes, beaches, sand dunes, beach ridges, and abandoned old pasture farmland.

Most unusual among these landscapes are silver maple swamps, which have a still, almost otherworldly feel to them, the spreading maples reflected in the calm surface of shallow ponds. The swamps and cattail marshes are important wildlife habitat, and, along with MacGregor Point's maple-beech forests, are home to such mammals as beaver, white-tailed deer, fox, snowshoe hare, racoon and porcupine. Weird and wonderful swamp and marsh critters include black-crowned night heron and great blue heron, watersnakes and shy painted turtles—and even carnivorous plants. Thirty species of butterflies have been recorded at MacGregor Point, including swallowtails, blues, brush-footed butterflies, browns, and several types of skippers.

MacGregor's visitors reap the reward of a cooperative conservation effort between the park and Ducks Unlimited. An extensive, rehabilitated marsh provides habitat for nesting and migrating ducks. Species nesting here include mallard, black duck, blue-winged and green-winged teal, Canada goose and wood ducks. The park's woodlands are also good for birding, with such species as great egret, red-bellied woodpecker and Carolina wren, Cape May warbler and gray-cheeked thrush.

Special Activities

MacGregor has some of the best cycling in Southwestern Ontario—traffic-free pathways through lovely dappled shade with a difficulty level suitable for family adventures. (Bike rentals available in Port Elgin.) The Old Shore Road Trail (6 km for hiking or biking) follows a former pioneer pathway between Goderich and Southampton. Old Shore is a pleasant ride past beaver ponds, beaches and shoreline and is a good connector between campgrounds and beaches. The Deer Run Bike Trail (1.6 km) is an ideal route between the campgrounds or beaches and the Lake Range Road (the main roadway to the park). Farther afield, it is easy to access the Lake Huron Shoreline Trail and Saugeen Rail Trail, which take you 12 km from the park to Southampton for a full day of sightseeing and cycling.

Hikers tread trails of their own. The Huron Fringe Trail (1.2 km, wheelchair accessible) has interpretive storyboards along its route that explain the special nature of dune vegetation, wetland formation, and local wildlife. The Lake Ridge Trail (4 km) is one of the more rigorous walks in the park. The trail follows the shoreline of glacial Lake Nipissing, and interesting features are described by storyboards: a pond created by beavers, a "corduroy" logging road and an abandoned homestead.

MacGregor Point's highlight is the 7-km Duck's Unlimited Trail (suitable for hiking or mountain biking). Cedar forest, swamp and ponds teem with wildlife most of the year, making a slow pace and binoculars much recommended. A viewing tower and boardwalks allow an up-close look at wildlife while keeping your feet dry.

Many campers make MacGregor their park of choice because of the two beaches, one of which has an excellent nautical-theme playground. A boat launch in nearby Port Elgin allows for even more fun on the waves, including fishing for trout, salmon or pickerel.

MacGregor Point Provincial Park has an active volunteer staff who maintain a visitor centre with a camper's library (stocked with field guides and other nature-oriented books), changing displays on local plants and animals, and a children's corner.

A regular schedule of events takes place throughout the camping season. The program includes a photography contest, guided hikes, and evening programs devoted to topics as diverse as birds of prey and medicinal plants. Especially popular are the August corn roast and the spring Huron Fringe Birding Festival. The entire family can join in on Saturday's campfire get-togethers.

During the winter, the park is open for use. Cross-country skiers use the ungroomed 3-km Nipissing Bluff Ski and snowmobilers travel along park roads.

Campground

MacGregor Point has plenty of space for its 360 campsites (107 electrical, many generously sized pull-through sites). These may be the largest and most private sites in Southern Ontario—and not a sub-standard site exists in the park. The campgrounds are laid out in cul-de-sacs, which reduces traffic levels. For families or small groups camping together, "paired" sites (two sites located close together) provide privacy and companionship. Sites 68 and 70 are yurt sites.

The three campgrounds are named Huron, Nipissing and Algonquin. The sites in Huron Campground tend to be more densely packed, although the following still provide superior privacy: the 279 to 285 loop (they are smaller sites), sites 290 and 293 (less undergrowth cover) and the excellent number 348. Nipissing Campround has several sites with excellent beach access, number 194 in particular. Nipissing's sites 184 to 186 are also better sites, while the following sites in the non-reservable section are especially recommended: 138, 143, 144, 136, 156, and 164. Algonquin Campground is close to the visitor centre; many of the sites here are pull-though electrical sites, which are among the best trailer sites in Ontario. For those wanting good beach access, sites 93, 117, 118 and 126 are good. The roadways in Algonquin are paved (read dust-free). All campgrounds have comfort stations with flush toilets and showers; laundry facilities are in Nipissing and Algonquin campgrounds only.

Local Attractions

Few provincial parks can boast the wide range of activities available nearby as can MacGregor Point. Rain or shine, there is something interesting to do in Port Elgin, Southampton or Kincardine. Southampton has shady streets of elegant Victorian homes and in the Bruce County Museum, a top-notch facility.

146

Kincardine also has a nice beach, an 1881 lighthouse-turned-museum with displays on local shipping, and wonderful fish restaurants. Fishing charters are available at the busy town marina. On Sunday evenings during the summer, a piper leads the town to Victoria Park for a band concert.

Port Elgin's beach is very active, geared towards the beach-volleyball set. Flea markets and carnivals frequently take place on the beach. A great daytrip can be made from Port Elgin through the protected bays and islands to Chantry Island with its much-photographed lighthouse. The trip is best taken via sea kayak; bring your own, or charter an entire guided trip from local outfitters.

Fast Facts

Campgrounds: 360 sites in three campgrounds (107 sites with hydro hookups); some sites wheelchair accessible. Group camping. Yurts available. Comfort stations with showers, laundry and flush toilets (accessible). Camping season: early May to mid-October. Reservations recommended for all sites all season.

Supplies: Firewood, ice and modest groceries sold in the park. Good grocery shopping in Port Elgin (6 km).

Facilities:

Trailer sanitation station

Trailer storage

Beach

Playground

Interpretive centre

Hiking trails (six trails totalling 19 km; one trail is wheelchair accessible)

Biking on several trails, and on long-distance trail from Port Elgin to Southampton

Winter Use: The park has a 3-km ungroomed ski trail. Snowmobiling is permitted on park roads.

Contact Information: RR 1, Port Elgin ON, N0H 2C5 tel 519-389-9056

Falls Reserve Conservation Area

Location: 2 km from the village of Benmiller,
   about 8 km southeast of Goderich off Roads 8 and 31.
Natural Environment: 1   Activities: 2   Campground: 1

Disney couldn't have designed a better waterpark than Mother Nature did along the Maitland River at Falls Reserve Conservation Area. A fortuitous combination of very warm, shallow water, porous bedrock and perfectly placed waterfalls rival any man-made facility. Away from the water, the park has spacious playing fields, a food concession and picnic areas, hiking trails and a fishpond. The surrounding region is prime touring country, with theatre, antique and art shops, and several good museums.

Natural Environment and History

In prehistoric times, the region including Huron County was covered by a warm inland sea. Sea dwellers, with their calcium-rich skeletons and shells, formed the basis of the sea bottom that became, over eons, bedrock. This porous rock is easily eroded into deep pockets and fissures by the rushing waters of the Maitland River. Every few hundred yards along the river is a pretty little waterfall. The river is not only scenic, but supports a healthy population of amphibians and fish. These creatures in turn attract heron, kingfishers, fox and racoons.

The history of the Maitland River is similar to that of the rest of Huron County, and this history is written on the landscape of the park. During the mid-1800s, loggers removed most of the forest cover and the cleared land became family farms. Thus, away from the river, Falls Reserve Conservation Area is largely fields reverting from pasture and cropland to natural meadow and young forest. Thousands of wildflowers bloom from May to October—aster, goldenrod, pearly everlasting, Queen Anne's lace, chicory, milkweed—and many more. These flowers, along with shrubs that follow them in succession, such as colourful sumac and mountain ash, attract field-dwelling species of sparrows, mice, rabbit, and predatory hawks and owls.

Special Activities

Although Falls Reserve is small, about 100 ha, it offers enormous family fun year-round. Bathtub-warm, ankle-deep water stretches from shore to

148

shore of the broad Maitland River. Pitted and grooved rock (water-smoothed for barefoot comfort) forms deeper pockets here and there, comfortable one-person whirlpools where you can sit submerged in sun-drenched water. The small waterfalls (about a half-metre in height) are yet another component of this waterpark. The water downstream of the waterfalls is deep enough to cushion the fall of any body surfer, but not too deep to frighten children. Just upstream from the cascades are deeper furrows in the bedrock that act as body-guiding channels perfectly aimed for the lip of the waterfall. No human ingenuity could have designed a better place for family fun.

Away from the river the park has sports fields galore, horseshoe pits, a playground, a food concession and walking paths. The paths are actually part of a much longer, 54-km route for hikers. In one direction, the paths lead through the park and eventually to the luxurious and historic Benmiller Inn. In the other direction, the paths lead upstream to join up with trails through the Morris Tract. In winter, these trails are beloved by cross-country skiers.

The Maitland River has an excellent fishery. Falls Reserve Conservation Area, in fact, boasts of year-round fishing for salmon. The park also has a small fishpond that is much enjoyed by beginning anglers.

The park organizes events several times daily during the summer and on weekends during the rest of the year. Hikes, campfires with sing-alongs, children's crafts and activities, and guest speakers and workshops are usual program components.

Campground

Falls Reserve has 163 campsites (125 electrical) in three campgrounds. None of the campgrounds provide much privacy, and most sites are very open, field sites. The best sites are in Mennestung Campground (although these sites are farthest from the river); in this campground, opt for sites numbered 27, 29 or 31. Some of the sites in Chippewa Campground are private from neighbouring sites, but are very open to the road. The best of these is number 12. The campground has a comfort station with showers and flush toilets but no laundry.

Local Attractions

Falls Reserve Conservation is close to the attractions of both Goderich and Bayfield. Much recommended sights in Goderich include the Huron County Pioneer Museum and the Huron County Historic Jail. The beautiful waterfront area, with its beach and much-heralded sunsets, are also worth a visit.

Farther south along Highway 21 is Bayfield, a daytripper's delight if ever there was one. Shops with wares as diverse as original art, women's high fashion, sporting goods and garden décor line the main street. The centrepiece of town is the Little Inn, with its excellent cuisine and historic picture-postcard charm.

Theatregoers will want to visit both Grand Bend and Blyth. Grand Bend's Huron Country Playhouse is housed in a restored barn and hosts light summertime comedy, mystery and drama. The Blyth Festival presents original Canadian works in a restored town hall.

Fast Facts

Campgrounds: 163 sites in three campgrounds (64 sites with hydro hookups); some sites wheelchair accessible. Group camping. Seasonal leasing. Comfort stations with showers, laundry, flush toilets (wheelchair accessible). Camping season mid-May to mid-October. Reservations recommended for all sites all summer long.

Supplies: Firewood sold in park. Good shopping available in Goderich (about 8 km).

Facilities:
Trailer sanitation station
Wading in the river
Playground
Sports fields
Horseshoe pits
Hiking trails (one trail connecting to 54 km)

Winter Use: The park is actively used for cross-country skiing. Trails here are part of a 54-km trail system.

Contact Information: Box 127, Wroxeter ON N0G 2X0
tel 519-335-3557

Pinery Provincial Park

Location: 6 km south of Grand Bend between
   Lake Huron and Highway 21.
Natural Environment: 2   Activities: 3   Campground: 1

Southern Ontario's largest park, the Pinery, is best known for its white
sand and lofty, tree-topped dunes, a sweet piece of uncrowded beach
on an otherwise busy Lake Huron shore. What many people don't
appreciate is that the park offers so much more, such as an oak savannah that is one of North America's rarest forest types. In addition, the
Pinery has good canoeing on picturesque backwaters rich with overhanging trees and fishing spots. The park also has several hiking trails
and kilometres of level cycling. The brand-new visitor centre has excellent displays on natural and human history and an equally good
nature-oriented shop.

Natural Environment and History

Sand, sand, as far as the eye can see. This is the remembrance most visitors have of the Pinery's 2,500 hectares. The 10-km-long beach, a mix of
sand and pebbles, has some of the better beachcombing possibilities in
Southern Ontario. Because the sands are not groomed, you can easily
find driftwood, net floats and other marine paraphernalia. The dunes rise
more than 30 m in height, and are topped with beach grasses, pine and
aspen. Park literature provides details on the hardy plants that colonize
the arid, shifting sands and stabilize the beach. Sand cherry, sea rocket,
ground juniper and little bluestem grass provide cover for the rare eastern hog nose snake.

Away from the beach, the Pinery's most important feature is the oak
savannah, an open forest of tall oak that cast a light shade over meadows
of grass and wildflowers such as orchids. This is as a very endangered
ecosystem: one-half of the savannah that remains on the continent is
located in this park. The park's long list of rare wildflowers include blue
hearts (it grows nowhere else in Canada) and the dense blazing star. The
Pinery is well known among birdwatchers, who travel here to spot prairie
warbler, red-headed woodpecker and whip-poor-will.

Another distinctive feature of the Pinery is its tranquil lagoons, the
remnant of an agricultural drainage canal called the Old Ausauble Channel, kept alive by seepage from underground springs. These still waters
are a perfect, unrippled mirror for the overhanging boughs and teem

151

with fish and birdlife. Many reptiles and amphibians also live near the channel: red-backed and blue-spotted salamanders, green snake, grey tree frog and five-lined skink.

Special Activities

A wide variety of ways exist for enjoying the Pinery's outstanding natural environment. Playing in the sand and out on the waves usually tops the list of many visitors. Boating, sailing and windsurfing on Lake Huron are also popular.

The park has 11 hiking trails of varying length; three of these are accessible to wheelchairs (Cedar, Heritage and Riverside). Long vistas over Lake Huron and the nearby Thedford Bog are the highlight of the 2-km Nipissing Trail. The rare oak savannah is best seen along the 2.3-km Cedar Trail, or from the Riverside Tail. Most trails have an explanatory brochure for a self-guiding interpretive experience.

The lagoons are best explored by canoe, and both canoes and paddleboats are rented at the park store. Fishermen cast a line in for bass or pike from the fishing platforms provided along the banks.

The park has a 14-km bike trail that winds through woods and meadow. Campers can access a bike path at the park's main gate that leads along a level and traffic-free route all the way to Grand Bend.

With such a large camper population to educate and entertain, park naturalists have a busy program of daily events. Guided hikes, evening hikes, children's puppet shows and crafts, movies and slide shows are commonly offered. During July and August the staff don costumes and perform the ever-popular "Rum and Spirits" presentation in the amphitheatre. The park also hosts group programs for school classes and other groups.

The park nature centre, newly completed, is a truly beautiful facility perched high on a knoll overlooking the forest. Changing displays and hands-on activities appeal to all ages. The Friends of Pinery run an excellent nature store with books, games, birdhouses, bat boxes, clothing and much more.

Winter visitors come to the park to use 30 km of cross-country ski trails with shelters and fireplaces. Walking trails are provided for snowshoers and hikers, so that optimum conditions are maintained on the ski trails. There is a specially designated area for wintertime fun with a toboggan hill and a heated chalet. The park rents skis and snowshoes and the park store sells light meals. Winter camping is increasingly popular at the Pinery.

Campground

This huge campground has 1,000 campsites (240 electrical). The sites are in three separate campgrounds, each densely spaced with little visual privacy. It can be quite congested on busy summer weekends. Burley and Dunes Campgrounds are closest to the beach, and Riverside Campground is located on the canal. Riverside area 4 is recommended for its less dense spacing and larger campsites. Numbers 692, 693, 829 and 830 may be the best of the lot. For those who want accommodation in yurts, the park rents four of these outfitted tents on platforms.

Local Attractions

The Pinery is located a scant 6 km south of Grand Bend, a summer fun town if ever there was one. Para-sailing, boating, sunbathing, beach volleyball, video arcades, and go-carts…and that's just the beginning. One of the highlights for campers is to bike to the south end of town and Best's Ice Cream's 26 homemade flavours. Another summer delight is the Huron County Playhouse, where cottagers and campers alike watch professional theatre in a huge and comfortably renovated barn.

Just across Highway 21 from the park is the Lambton Heritage Museum. The museum has a pioneer home, general store and school, as well as several agricultural buildings and antique equipment. The museum building houses changing displays on local history. Of particular interest are two collections: pressed-glass decanters and vases, and historic lithographs. The museum almost always has a well-run event going on, from a celebration of the returning swans to an antique auto rally.

Fast Facts

Campgrounds: 1,000 sites in two campgrounds (404 sites with hydro hookups); some sites wheelchair accessible. Group camping. Yurts available. Comfort stations with showers, flush toilets and laundries (wheelchair accessible). Camping season from early April to mid-October. Reservations recommended for all sites on May long weekend and from mid-June to September.

Supplies: Firewood and ice sold in park. Park store sells groceries and ice cream. Best shopping in Grand Bend (6 km).

Facilities:

Trailer sanitation station

Trailers/boat storage

Canoe/kayak launch

Canoe, paddleboat and bike rentals

Beach
Playground
Visitor centre
Hiking trails (10 trails totalling 17 km; one trail is
    wheelchair accessible)
Winter Use: The park is open all winter and has extensive cross-country
    trails (30 km) and tobogganing.
Contact Information: RR 2, Grand Bend ON, N0P 2P0
    tel 519-243-2220

Rondeau Provincial Park

Location: 33 km south of Chatham on Lake Erie. Access from Road 17.
Natural Environment: 2   Activities: 2   Campground: 1

Ontario's Deep South: immense trees growing in lush, viny woodlands;
tropically hued birds; possums, fox snakes and other unusual critters.
One of Ontario's rarest habitat types is Carolinian forest, home to plants
and animals normally found in the southeast United States. Although
development destroyed all but 10 percent of the original Carolinian forest, the largest area of remaining southern hardwoods is protected within
Rondeau Provincial Park. Park naturalists host a varied education program to highlight this remarkably beautiful environment. The park has
many other attractions: beaches; good conditions for boating, sailing and
windsurfing; and kilometres of level cycling.

Natural Environment and History

Rondeau's 3,200 ha boast a remarkable diversity of habitat types: marshes, pebble and sand beaches, forest (pine-oak and maple-beech), wooded
sloughs and sand dunes. The reason for this natural richness lies in the
geologic past. Rondeau is a peninsula (one of the world's best examples
of a "cuspate sandspit," according to geologists) created during millennia
of glaciation. The Lake Erie side of the peninsula was constantly built up
by sand eroded from cliffs east and west of the peninsula. The constant
rising and falling of Lake Erie created a series of parallel ridges and
depressions along the peninsula. These depressions are now wooded
sloughs that are habitat for countless creatures.

Ontarians familiar with forest hikes elsewhere in the province never fail to gasp at the very different ambience at Rondeau. The trees here are huge, especially the shagbark hickories; one needs to look way up very straight trunks to catch a glimpse of leaves far above the canopy. The forest floor is covered with ferns, moss and other moisture-lovers. The sense of luxuriant growth is almost palpable; it seems anything that remains still for a few days starts to turn green. The list of rare plants found at Rondeau reads like a who's who of Ontario botany: sassafras, tulip tree, black gum, flowering dogwood, orchids (19 species), oswego tea and tall bellflower.

Southern animals, too, thrive in Rondeau's climate of warm winters and plentiful summer rainfall. Opossum, southern flying squirrels, and red-headed woodpecker are among the uncommon species that live in the park, along with deer, racoons and coyote. Birdwatchers from far and wide thrill at a glimpse of a prothonotory or a cerulean warbler. Over 80 percent of the birds you can see in Ontario may be observed at Rondeau.

The expansive marshes are also very worthwhile for naturalists, especially during spring and fall when Rondeau is used as an important resting and feeding ground for ducks, geese, rails, bitterns and herons. Whistling swans visit the marsh annually in March and early April during migration. The bald eagle, once almost extirpated along Lake Erie, is making a healthy comeback at Rondeau, and several aeries—huge stick-nests built by eagles and reused each year—are visible from the marsh. The marsh is also habitat for reptiles and amphibians. Spotted, Blanding's and spiny soft-shell turtles live at Rondeau, as do Fowler's toads, hog-nose snake and fox snake. Another herptile with celebrity status is the five-lined skink, Ontario's only lizard.

The long beach and sand dunes, too, have their enthusiasts among naturalists. Birdwatchers study migrating gulls, terns, sandpipers and plovers. Botanists identify such drought-hardy plants as sand cherry, little bluestem, sea rocket and yellow puccoon.

Such natural riches attract economic development. Since Ontario's early history, commercial fishing, forestry, trapping and hunting were important activities at Rondeau. Farming is now the main economic activity in the area, although a commercial fishery operates from nearby Erieau.

Special Activities

Rondeau offers visitors many different ways to enjoy its distinctive environment. The park has five nature trails. The following three trails are not suitable for cycling. Woodland sloughs are best seen along the Tulip Tree

Trail (1.5 km of barrier-free design), and birding is great along the Spice-bush Trail (1.5 km). Drier pine-oak forest is the attraction along the 1.4-km Black Oak Trail. Three trails are longer ventures and are suitable for walking or cycling. The 14-km Marsh Trail stretches along the entire bay side of the peninsula, and is an excellent outing for spotting heron, bittern, frogs and snakes. South Point Trail is a trip through southern woodlands, and is a more quiet, lesser-used route. The park's level road-ways are also excellent for cycling or roller-blading.

Fishing by boat on Lake Erie and by canoe in the marsh are popular outings here. The most-sought species are bass, pike and famous Lake Erie yellow perch. Ice fishing also takes place at Rondeau. Canoe rentals are available just outside the park, and the channels through the marsh are ideal for quiet nature study. Boat rentals and launching facilities are also just outside the park. Sailing lessons are available at Rondeau Yacht Club.

In recent years, the reputation of Rondeau Bay for windsurfing has grown, and enthusiasts can be seen on the water from early spring to late fall. In their wake are photographers, who find sparkling blue waters and bright sails a winning combination. The 12-km beach along Lake Erie is perfect for volleyball, sunbathing and swimming.

Given the park's unique plants and animals, it is appropriate that the visitor program be nature-oriented. The new visitor centre has displays on Rondeau's flora and fauna. Events take place daily during the summer and on spring and fall weekends. Children's programs, evening movies and slide talks, guided hikes and canoe outings and campfires take place several times a week. Special weekend programs include spring bird-watching weekends, natural gardening workshops, colour tours and a Christmas sale.

Campground

Rondeau's 258 campsites are in an open, almost tree-less field. In addi-tion, the campground can be very dusty in droughty years, and the grass can be pretty worn. However, if you are camping at Rondeau, you will want to know that the best site is number 194.

The campground has comfort stations with wheelchair-accessible toilets, showers and laundry. Convenient access to the beach from the campground is by way of short pathways.

Local Attractions

Rondeau is about an hour drive from Point Pelee National Park. (See Wheatley Provincial Park.) Pelee is the best place to birdwatch in Cana-da, and is of great interest to those who study plants, insects, reptiles and amphibians. Any naturalist camping at Rondeau will want to visit Pelee for a day.

The Greenview Aviaries are located near Blenheim, where there are dozens of caged tropical birds, from parrots to toucans, as well as emu and rhea. This is a good place for young children, who enjoy an excellent playground and plenty of opportunities to feed animals.

Farther afield in Dresden (north of Chatham) is the Uncle Tom's Cabin Museum. Several buildings include the home and church built by Josiah Henson, model for Stowe's Uncle Tom. The museum focuses on the black fugitives who settled in Southwestern Ontario in communities such as Dresden. An excellent museum for all ages.

fast facts

Campground: 258 campsites in one campground (152 sites with hydro hookups); some sites wheelchair accessible. Group camping. Comfort stations with showers, flush toilets and laundries (all wheelchair accessible). Camping season year-round. Reservations recommended for all sites all summer long and for all long weekends.

Supplies: Firewood and ice sold in park. Park store has modest grocery shopping and ice cream stand. Better shopping available in Morpeth (10 km).

Facilities:

Trailer sanitation station

Boat launch but no docking (marinas just outside park entrance)

Beach (parking, barbecues, comfort stations)

Interpretive centre

Hiking (five trails totalling over 26 km some trails are wheelchair accessible)

Winter Use: The park is open all winter and there is cross-country skiing on the hiking trails.

Contact Information: RR 1, Morpeth ON, N0P 1X0 tel 519-674-1750

Wheatley Provincial Park

Location: 13 km east of Leamington on Lake Erie.
   Access from Highway 3.
Natural Environment: 1   Activities: 2   Campground: 3

Southwestern Ontario beckons to travellers with a multiplicity of experiences—wine tours, birdwatching, beachcombing, fall fairs and exceptional museums, to name but a few. Wheatley Provincial Park near Kingsville is a well-situated base camp for rewarding regional visits. Wheatley's campgrounds, among the best in Southwestern Ontario, are located in verdant forest resplendent with wildflowers each spring and home to plants and animals usually found much farther south on the continent. A modest interpretive program highlights such flora and fauna as shagbark hickory and fox snake. Campers enjoy swimming on a fine beach, canoeing and fishing.

Natural Environment and History

Wheatley's 240 ha include several provincially significant habitat types. Most famous is the Carolinian forest, named because it harbours species normally found in the southeastern United States. Wheatley (along with Rondeau Provincial Park and Pelee National Park) is one of the largest remaining tracts of Carolinian forest that remains in Southwestern Ontario. Of these three parks, only Wheatley offers the only opportunity to actually live within southern forest.

Wheatley is known particularly for its large shagbark hickories, very tall, straight trees named for their unusual bark that hangs in ragged strips. The park also protects a small area of oak savannah, an extension of the great American plains eco-region that has a toehold in the extreme southwest of Ontario. Wheatley is unusual in that its wildflowers are perhaps more talked about than its forest giants. The campgrounds, as well as the hiking trails, host a breathtaking springtime bloom that brings photographers from far and wide. Cardinal flower, orchids and wild bergamot share the park with cinnamon fern, shining club moss, spike-rush and bluestem grasses.

In addition to forest, Wheatley has a large area of creek and marshlands, habitat for great blue heron, egrets, painted and snapping turtles and fox snake. These tranquil creeks are valuable, sheltered areas used as refuges by migrating ducks and geese. Wheatley's Lake Erie shoreline is also a migratory stopover, a haven for gulls, terns, and sandpipers.

Special Activities

Each of Wheatley's habitat types can be enjoyed in a different way. Hiking trails, and even park roadways, bring visitors into direct contact with the myriad species of wildflowers. Two short, unnamed trails (each about one kilometre in length) include footbridges over the creeks and along the shoreline of Lake Erie.

The creeks and marshes are best enjoyed by canoe, and these quiet waters are an excellent place for novices to strengthen their skills. By canoe, you can get good looks at exotic egrets, sunning turtles and other elusive creatures. A convenient canoe launch is provided on Boosey Creek, and canoe rentals are available just outside the park.

Wheatley's 2-km sand beach is perfect for swimming and sunbathing. Boaters and sailors make use of a boat ramp at Wheatley Harbour to depart for the open waters of Lake Erie. Yellow perch are the attraction for many fishermen on the lake. The park's creeks are fished for catfish, carp and panfish.

Although Wheatley does not have a regular interpretive program, the park hosts several special events each year, including a springtime birding tour, a summertime fishing derby and a fall migration festival. Children's craft programs are often organized by the campground host; please ask at the park gate for information.

Campground

Wheatley's 220 campsites are situated in four campgrounds. In general, the sites are larger and more spread out than sites found in other parks in Southwestern Ontario. Some of the more secluded and quiet sites are located in the Boosey Creek Campground; the best sites here are numbers 3, 14, 30, 34, 38 to 41 and 49. The sites in Highlands Campground are secluded but tend to be grassy rather than forested. Middle Creek Campground, conveniently located near a footbridge to the beaches, has sites that are more crowded and open. All electrical sites are in Middle Creek Campground. Two Creeks Campground has many sites with waterfront access; some of the best are numbers 184, 186 and 198. The park has comfort stations with flush toilets and laundries.

Local Attractions

Wheatley is only a few kilometres from Point Pelee National Park, one of the "hottest" birding spots in North America. Although the birdwatching (and botanizing) at Pelee is excellent year-round, the park is most famous for the springtime invasion of warblers, thrushes, birds of prey, gulls, terns…and countless others. September is the time to see Monarch butterflies rest in great numbers waiting for the right time to continue their southward migration.

Just west of Point Pelee lies Kingsville, a favourite haunt of nature lovers because it is the location of the Jack Miner Bird Sanctuary. Revered Jack Miner, father of Canadian conservation, used the family farm to establish a sanctuary for migrating waterfowl, entertain the elite from several continents, and spearhead campaigns for restrictions on hunting. The Sanctuary has plenty of geese to watch and feed year-round, but it is autumn when hundreds of people gather to watch thousands of Canada geese take to the air each afternoon. The small but excellent museum on site is devoted to Miner's achievements.

Harrow has several sites of interest. Wine tours and tastings take place at Pelee Island Winery (despite the name, it is located on the main-land) and Colio Wines. Colasanti Tropical Gardens is a magnet for green thumbs year-round (and draws those who long for warmth and the scent of growing things from October to March). The expansive greenhouses are filled with foliage plants, orchids, lilies and cacti of every description.

The best museum in the area is the North American Black Historical Museum in Amherstburg. Historic documents, maps and videos tell the story of the Underground Railroad, the route used by fugitive slaves who escaped to live their lives in Southwestern Ontario.

Fast Facts

Campgrounds: 220 sites in four campgrounds (89 sites with hydro
hookups); some sites are wheelchair accessible. Group camping.
Comfort stations with showers and flush toilets (wheelchair accessible). Camping season from early April to mid-October.
Reservations recommended for all sites on long weekends
and during July and August.

Supplies: Firewood and ice sold in the park. Shopping in Wheatley (2 km).

Facilities:
Trailer sanitation station
Beach
Hiking (two trails totalling 2 km)
Boat launch

Winter Use: The park is gated in the winter, but walkers and skiers can
still use the trails.

Contact Information: Box 640, Wheatley ON, N0P 2P0
tel 519-825-4659

Port Burwell Provincial Park

Location: 26 km south of Tillsonburg on Lake Erie.
   Access from Road 19.
Natural Environment: 2   Activities: 1   Campground: 2

An easy way to start a spirited debate is to ask a group of Ontarians to name the best of the province's Great Lakes beaches. An easy way to finish the debate is to take everyone to Port Burwell Provincial Park, the least-appreciated beach, but very likely the best of the lot. Port Burwell's beach is huge—both broad and long—and is never crowded. Lake Erie supplies large waves in abundance and constant cooling breezes. The park's campground has sites that are well spaced out, a modest interpretive program, sports fields galore and a hiking trail.

Natural Environment and History

Port Burwell is not a large park, at 227 hectares, but it does contain a variety of landscape types. About 12,000 years ago the region lay underneath a glacial lake. The sediment deposited under the lake is the origin of the soft, sandy soil of surrounding Norfolk County. The sand dunes and bluffs along the beach are formed by modern Lake Erie as wind and waves constantly erode and deposit soil. The sandy soil of Norfolk is easily eroded, and so streams and rivers quickly form steep ravines. Indeed, wooded ravines are one of the most noticeable features of lands near Lake Erie.

It is interesting that the park's most significant feature, its beach, is actually changing almost daily. Wave action changes the sandbars with every swell. The back dunes are actually rapidly increasing in height, the increase aided by rehabilitation programs such as the construction of a break wall.

The forest here has many species of plants normally found in the southern United States, such as sassafras, oak, blue beech and Virginia bluebells. Correspondingly southern animals found at Port Burwell include Acadian flycatcher, Carolina wren, badger and opossum. The park is known for its spring wildflower blooms and throngs of migrating songbirds.

Special Activities

The main draw at Port Burwell is the splendid beach. Because this 2-km strand is very broad and edged with tall dunes, the cars and parking lots are kept a good distance from the shoreline. Indeed, it is easy to forget that life away from the beach exists at all, especially on days when Erie's surf roars loudly. The beach has ample room for all types of play, from volleyball to castle building. Each of the five beach areas is equally recommended. While you can wade far out into Lake Erie at all beaches, Beach 3 has the largest area of ankle-deep water preferred by toddlers. There's also a nearby food concession, and for those who prefer shade with their sand, large trees at the leeward edge of the beach provide plenty of cool shade.

One of the charms of Port Burwell is that the waves are consistently large, and the water temperature is dependably warm. Combined with shallow waters and multiple sandbars, this is a water playground par excellence. Lake Erie is notorious for undertows and rip tides during rough weather. Take the time to review safety precautions for swimming at Port Burwell.

Away from the beach are facilities for baseball, badminton, volleyball and horseshoes. Sports equipment for any of these activities may be borrowed from the park office. The park has a one-kilometre hiking trail. The aptly named Ravine Creek Trail follows a steep ravine cut into the sandy soil by a small creek. Along the path one may observe plenty of wildlife, from blue jays to painted turtles. The vegetation is mature hardwood forest, pine plantation and several types of wild berries. All-terrain wheelchairs are available for use on the trail. Longer hikes and bike rides are taken along the 30-km "Rails to Trails" path that begins near the park. Park roads are also suitable for cycling.

Port Burwell has several good places to fish, including Big Otter Creek, Port Burwell Harbour and Lake Erie. Species commonly sought include channel catfish, sheepshead, carp and yellow perch.

Campground

Port Burwell Provincial Park has 232 campsites, and 117 of these have hydro hookups. Each of the park's three campgrounds (Leander, Iroquois and Alzora) have a comfort station with flush toilets, showers and a laundry. Leander Campground is closest to the playground and sports fields.

This park has some of the best campsites in Southern Ontario. Although many campsites are sheltered by good shrubbery screens, many sites are open to the roadway. No sites have direct beach access. In fact, most campsites are about 2 km from the beach, and thus most campers drive to the beach. The best campsites are numbers 39, 41, 42, to 44 and 46. These sites have the best privacy, and are closest to the beach.

Church services are held in the campground on Sundays during July and August.

Local Attractions

Nature-lovers will want to head for two local sites. Trillium Woods Provincial Park (a day-use facility) near Sweaburg has a splendid bloom of our provincial wildflower in May. The park is known for the unusual colour variations in the trilliums that thrive here—from purple to green and striped varieties. September through November is the time to visit Hawk Cliff (west of Port Burwell on the lakeshore) for observing birds of prey, including falcons and eagles, as they migrate.

Some sites of historic interest are close to the park. The Port Burwell lighthouse (1840) is open to the public; you can climb to the top for views of the town and the beach. Just across the street is the Port Burwell Marine Museum, which has displays of artifacts and documents describing local history. The town of Vienna is home to a museum devoted to the life and accomplishments of Thomas Edison; displays include one of the inventor's original light bulbs.

Green thumbs love to study the waterlilies and aquatic life at Reimer's Waterscapes. A variety of water gardens, from small tubs to huge ponds, are stocked with everything needed to re-create a backyard Eden.

Fast Facts

Campgrounds: 232 sites in three campgrounds (117 sites with electrical hookups); some sites wheelchair accessible. Group camping. Comfort stations with showers, laundry, flush toilets (wheelchair accessible). Camping season mid-May to mid-October. Reservations recommended for all sites from late May to early September.

Supplies: Firewood and ice sold in park. The park has a food concession. Groceries available in Port Burwell just outside park.

Facilities:
Trailer sanitation station
Trailer/boat storage
Boat launch near the park
Beach
Playground
Sports fields
Hiking trails (one trail totalling one km)

Winter Use: The park is closed in winter.

Contact Information: Box 9, Port Burwell ON, N0J 1T0
tel 519-874-4691

Elora Gorge Conservation Area

Location: 25 km northwest of Guelph on Road 21;
   adjacent to the village of Elora.
Natural Environment: 2   **Activities:** 2   **Campground:** 1

The Grand River, designated a National Heritage River because of its primary role in Ontario's development, is the longest, deepest and fastest-flowing river in the southwestern part of the province. The most scenic stretch of the Grand flows downstream from the historic village of Elora, where 90-metre-high cedar-shrouded cliffs channel the river and increase the velocity sufficiently to allow for inner-tubing. The Elora Gorge Conservation Area offers riverside recreation year-round, from springtime's fishing through summer's hiking to winter's cross-country skiing. The campsites here serve well as a convenient base for exploring several country villages.

Natural Environment and History

The Elora Gorge Conservation Area is 142 ha in area, a long, narrow strip of land on either side of the Grand River. The river has done an admirable job of sculpting its deep limestone canyon into weird shapes, overhanging ledges, caves and caverns. The forest along the cliff tops is predominantly mature cedar, and the cliff face has enough ferns, lichens and mosses to keep botanists busy.

The Grand River itself varies dramatically with the seasons, from spring's noisy whitewater to late summer's river of clear, shallow brown water. Winter brings its own sparkling beauty to the park, and many a photographer has been kept busy composing a winning combination of cliff-hugging icicles and snow-draped cedars.

Special Activities

The Elora Gorge Conservation Area is made for year-round fun. The kilometres of hiking trails travel through cedar-scented groves along the verge of the cliffs. The trails lead from the bridge at the upstream end of the park right into the village of Elora. The most popular length of path includes Hole in the Wall (a cave with winding staircase), some scenic overlooks, and a couple of steep descents to sheltered coves where kayakers take a break before heading further down the river.

There's no better way to handle summer's heat than inner-tubing on the Grand. Bring your own equipment, or rent some for reasonable rates at the concession in the park. A remarkably pleasant day can be had enjoying the variety of exhilarating rapid runs and the intermittent slow, swirling stretches of water—part lazy river and part waterslide. A convenient shuttle service operates during peak summer periods to carry tubers and tubes from the lower park back to the starting point. All inner-tubers must register at the beachhouse near the front gate.

The park has a small swimming pond (one hectare), a concession stand and a camp store with basic supplies. The day-use area of the park has several sports facilities: horseshoe pits, volleyball and basketball courts, baseball diamonds, a playground and a football field.

The Grand River is one of Ontario's hot spots for fly-fishing, and the river is stocked with brown trout. Some portions of the Grand in and around the Elora Conservation Area are designated for catch-and-release practices.

Elora is also busy during the winter, a great time of year to enjoy the gorge when it is peaceful. Ten kilometres of marked and track-set cross-country ski trails are suitable for novice and intermediate skiers. Ski rentals are available at the park, as are washrooms and unserviced winter camping (reservations required).

Campground

This is a huge campground, with 550 campsites (210 with hydro and water), as well as seven group camping areas. Some sites may be leased on a monthly or seasonal basis. Given the large number of sites, the high density of campers and the level of noise and activity experienced on summer weekends, choosing a good site is rather difficult.

The campground has several sections, a chief distinction between them being their location south of the river or north of the river. Camping areas north of the river (Sections D to H) tend to be somewhat larger and less congested then areas south of the river (Sections A to C); the latter are closer to the swimming pond, hiking trails and the camp store. Areas A and B, E and F are noisy and densely packed with little visual privacy. Section C has serviced sites and trailer sites, and of these, sites 166, 170, 194 and 197 are best. Section D has some sites that are convenient for inner-tubers who want to be close to their ending point (sites 249 to 251). Section G is reserved for group camping. Section H has some of the better sites, particular numbers 482 and 483, as well as sites 489 to 495.

Local Attractions

It is an easy walk from the campground to Elora, well known for its dozens of interesting boutiques, galleries and restaurants in historic limestone buildings. The venerable stone Elora Mill Inn stands at the end of Mill Street. The Mill's restaurant and pub have the best view of the village symbol, the Tooth of Time, a limestone islet that stands in the centre of a waterfall at the head of the gorge. The village hosts the Elora Festival, three weeks of performances by renowned choirs and other musicians in unusual venues, such as a floating platform in the Elora Quarry. The Elora-Cataract Trail (47 km) connects Elora with the towns of Fergus and Hillsburgh before reaching the scenic Forks of the Credit. The trail is open to walkers, bikers and cross-country skiers.

Scottish Fergus is also a pretty Grand River town, and it too, has an excellent restaurant and pub in the Breadalbane Inn. Each August tens of thousands visit Fergus for the Highland Games and its competitions in dance, pipe bands and athletics. The Grand Theatre presents professional theatre during the summer, and a variety of jazz and other events during the fall and winter.

Between Elora and Fergus is the Elora Quarry Conservation Area. This abandoned limestone quarry provides wonderfully cool, deep-water swimming (unsuitable for young children). Just down the road is the landmark Wellington County Museum and Archives, a facility that is part local history museum and part art gallery. The museum hosts many special events year-round, such as garden parties and antique auto shows.

Fast Facts

Campgrounds: 550 campsites in eight campgrounds (210 sites with both hydro and water hookups); some wheelchair accessible sites. Group camping. Seasonal leasing. Comfort stations with showers, laundry, flush toilets (accessible). Camping season late April to late October. Reservations recommended for hydro sites all season and for all sites on weekends.

Supplies: Firewood and ice sold in the park. Food concession in park. Shopping in Elora (adjacent to park).

Facilities:

    Trailer sanitation station

    Seasonal storage of trailers

    Inner-tube rentals

    Beach

    Playground

    Hiking trails (two trails totalling 8 km)

Winter Use: The park is open all winter and has 10 km of cross-country ski trails. There are ski rentals, a warm-up hut and unserviced winter camping.

Contact Information: Box 356, Elora ON, N0B 1S0 tel 519-846-9742